The weaver, the shoemaker and the mother of a nation

The story of Dorking's *Mayflower* Pilgrims

Kathy Atherton and Susannah Horne

with additional research by Jane le Cluse

Mullins Mayflower 400

THE COCKEREL PRESS

The weaver, the shoemaker and the mother of a nation

First published in 2019 by The Cockerel Press

Copyright © 2019 Kathy Atherton and Susannah Horne

All rights reserved. No part of this publication may be reproduced, stored in an electronic retrieval system, or transmitted, in any form, or by any means, electronic, mechanical, photocopying, recording or otherwise, without the prior written permission of the publisher and copyright holder.

ISBN 978-1-909871-18-2

The Cockerel Press is an imprint of
Dorking Museum and Heritage Centre, The Old Foundry, 62 West Street, Dorking RH4 1BS
www.dorkingmuseum.org.uk
Enquiries to admin@dorkingmuseum.org.uk

Printed and bound by Short Run Press Limited, Exeter

We acknowledge the use of public sector information from the National Archives licensed under the Open Government Licence v3.0. All efforts have been made to contact copyright holders of images contained in this book. Please get in touch with The Cockerel Press if you hold copyright to an un-credited image so that this can be acknowledged in later editions.

Contents

Acknowledgments and Thanks   3

A fine house in 'Darking'   4
A new found land   20
'Saints' and 'strangers'   22
The *Mayflower* – 'meat for fishes'   24
The Mayflower Compact   28
'An unknown coast'   32
'A hideous and desolate wilderness'   38
'Why don't you speak for yourself, John?'   44
Populating the colony   50

Appendix 1 – The *Mayflower* Passenger List   60
Appendix 2 – The Will of William Mullins   62
Appendix 3 – Peter Browne and William Mullins: Summary of Caleb Johnson's research   64
Appendix 4 - Map of central Dorking showing the location of key 17th century buildings and surviving structures   79

Bibliography   82
Index   84

Acknowledgments and Thanks

This book has drawn on the research of many individuals over many years. Special acknowledgement is due to Dorking Local History Group for the initial research into the Mullins family and to Beryl Higgins and the Domestic Buildings Research Group for research on the house. This has been followed up by Caleb Johnson, from the United States, who convincingly pinned *Mayflower* voyager Peter Browne to Dorking in 2004. Many thanks to Caleb and to Nathaniel L Taylor of The American Genealogist for allowing us to reprint his findings in detail and to Jane le Cluse for her efforts in trying to establish the reason for William Mullins' troubles with the law and for the transcription of his will. Alicia Crane Williams and Desiree Mobed of the Alden Kindred of America have provided invaluable insights, as has Dr Tom McCarthy of the US Naval Academy. Thanks to Tom Loftus for producing the map, to Roy Williamson for his stunning photographs. Without any of these the book would be much poorer. Julian Womersley rendered invaluable service during the editing process and, as ever, Peter Camp has quietly overseen the publication process.

William Mullins' House, now known as 58-60 West Street and housing several businesses, in 2019. The extension to the right is a later addition. (Image Royston Williamson)

A fine house in 'Darking'

A handsome jettied building stands in the middle of Dorking's West Street, not far from Pump Corner. It is the only home of a 'Pilgrim Father' that is known to have survived into the 21st century. The life of its owner, William Mullins, is celebrated by a blue plaque on the front of the building. Yet Mullins was just one of six Dorking residents to travel to the New World on the *Mayflower*: at least three more later joined them in the colony and another five had crossed to New England by the 1640s.

So who made up that first Dorking contingent? What were their lives in the town like before 1620? Why did they leave the place of their birth on a perilous journey to an uncertain future? What happened to

William Mullins' house on West Street drawn in 1907. (Drawing by AC Fare from the collection of Dorking Museum)

them on arrival in the New World? The 'Thanksgiving' feast enjoyed by the colonists after bringing in their first harvest is world famous but fewer than half of these individuals from a small and rather isolated country town were to survive the events that made that celebration so poignantly symbolic. This book tells the story of those first Dorking 'Pilgrims'.

Dorking's best-known 'Pilgrim Father', William Mullins, was born in the Surrey market town in about 1572. He was the son of John Mullins and his wife Joan, née Bridger. We do not know if the Mullinses were a local family or much about young William's early life in the town, save that he and his brother, John, like their father, went into the shoemaking business. As a youth, he would have been obliged to practise his long-bow skills on the common known as Cotmandene on Sunday after church, on pain of a fine if he played dice or bowls instead.

The weaver, the shoemaker and the mother of a nation

A fashionable 17th century child's shoe was found placed up a chimney in South Street during renovations in the 1980s. It would have been put there to ward off evil spirits. It has been dated to the later 17th century, some time after Mullins had left on the *Mayflower*, but would not have been very different from the shoes that Mullins took with him to the new colony. In the period it was believed that doorways, thresholds and chimneys were weak points in a building's structure through which evil spirits might enter and that placing worn items which bore traces of human imprint, particularly shoes, in those locations would attract the spirits to them rather than to the human occupants. (Photograph by Royston Williamson, from the collection of Dorking Museum)

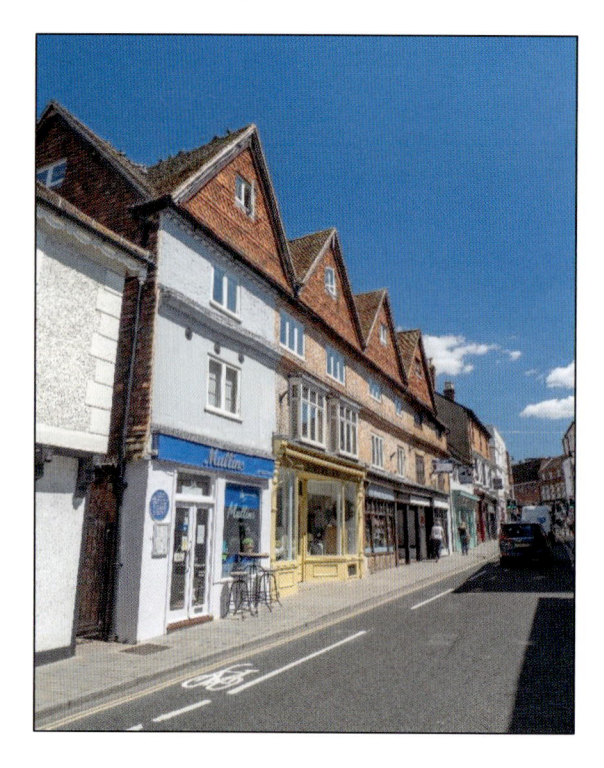

Mullins' House looking east along West Street, with the coffee shop that is named after the family in the nearest of the four bays of the building. (Image Royston Williamson)

He was fined 2d in October 1595, whilst in his twenties; not for playing dice but for failing to attend a session of the Dorking manorial courts. He seems to have left Dorking for a time after this, possibly to live near Guildford; he returned to live in the centre of Dorking as a married man with children. The fact that Mullins' marriage and the baptisms of his children are not to be found in the Dorking parish registers has been taken to suggest that he might have been a dissenter from the Church of England. However, the records are incomplete for the years when Mullins was bringing up his family and the fact that he had considerable status in the community, standing as witness and executor for various wills, does not suggest any overt radicalism. By 1604, he had been elected to the responsible position of 'tithingman' for Eastborough, representing his family and neighbours. Once he returned from Guildford, he was certainly prosperous enough to buy a property in Dorking for £122 on 28th December 1612.

The house that William Mullins bought had belonged to the Sheffield family, who owned large amounts of land in the Dorking area. It stood on West Street. A few yards to the east lay Pump Corner, a source of drinking water in the heart of the town's commercial district. There had been a house on the site since at least the 1490s but the property now known as 'Mullins' House' is thought to have been built on the site of the original house between the later years of the 16th century and 1619. It is possible that Mullins was responsible for the rebuilding. Whoever commissioned it, it was a prestigious building: four timber-framed, gabled houses, formed a terrace, each with a jetty overhanging the street and its own separate entrance. Such terraces would usually have been built for rent with the lower floors used as shops or workshops and living accommodation above.

When he bought the house in West Street, (also taking over the existing mortgage of £200), Mullins was not only married but had fathered at least four children: Joseph and Priscilla, who accompanied their father to America eight years later, and William and Sarah, who remained in England. We do not know if Mullins' wife Alice was the mother of all the children or if theirs was a second marriage; if it was, she may only have been the mother of Joseph, the youngest child.

It is likely that Mullins and his family only occupied one unit of the property, selling shoes from the ground floor and letting out the rest. It was a large property for a shoemaker to have been able to afford, which suggests that either Mullins had done very well in business (and was now a trader in shoes, rather than a skilled shoemaker) or that his wife Alice brought money to the marriage, enabling him to invest in the property. The two may have married shortly before the purchase; certainly, their son Joseph was born not too long afterwards. Baby Joseph and his older sister (or half-sister) Priscilla probably spent most of their childhoods in the house on West Street. From there they could walk to the water pump at the end of the road or past the tithe barn down to the communal washing place on the Pipp brook which ran behind St Martin's Church.

The Mullinses were not the only Dorking residents to travel on the *Mayflower*. American researcher Caleb Johnson has conclusively shown that the man named Peter Browne listed among the passengers also came from the town. Born in the mid-1590s, Browne was one of six children of William Browne of Dorking, most of whom had been apprenticed as weavers on their father's death. We do not know where Browne lived, but his cousins owned two tenements and a garden on South Street, in the area now occupied by the Spotted Dog. It is likely that Browne heard of the opportunity to travel through his connection with the Mullins family. Dorking was a small town and there is plenty of evidence that Browne would have known the family: his older sister Jane had married into the Hammon family and William Mullins had been appointed executor of her mother-in-law's will. When Mullins sold his property in Dorking, it was to the husband of Jane Browne's sister-in-law, Ephraim Bothell. Caleb Johnson also speculates that William Mullins' wife, Alice, may have been the widow of a man named Thomas Browne. If that is correct, the Mullins family might have had an even closer relationship with Peter Browne – quite possibly Alice Mullins was his aunt.

A drawing of a horse, thought to date from the period 1590-1610, was found inside the Mullins' House during refurbishments in 2011. (Image reproduced by permission of Surrey Domestic Buildings Research Group)

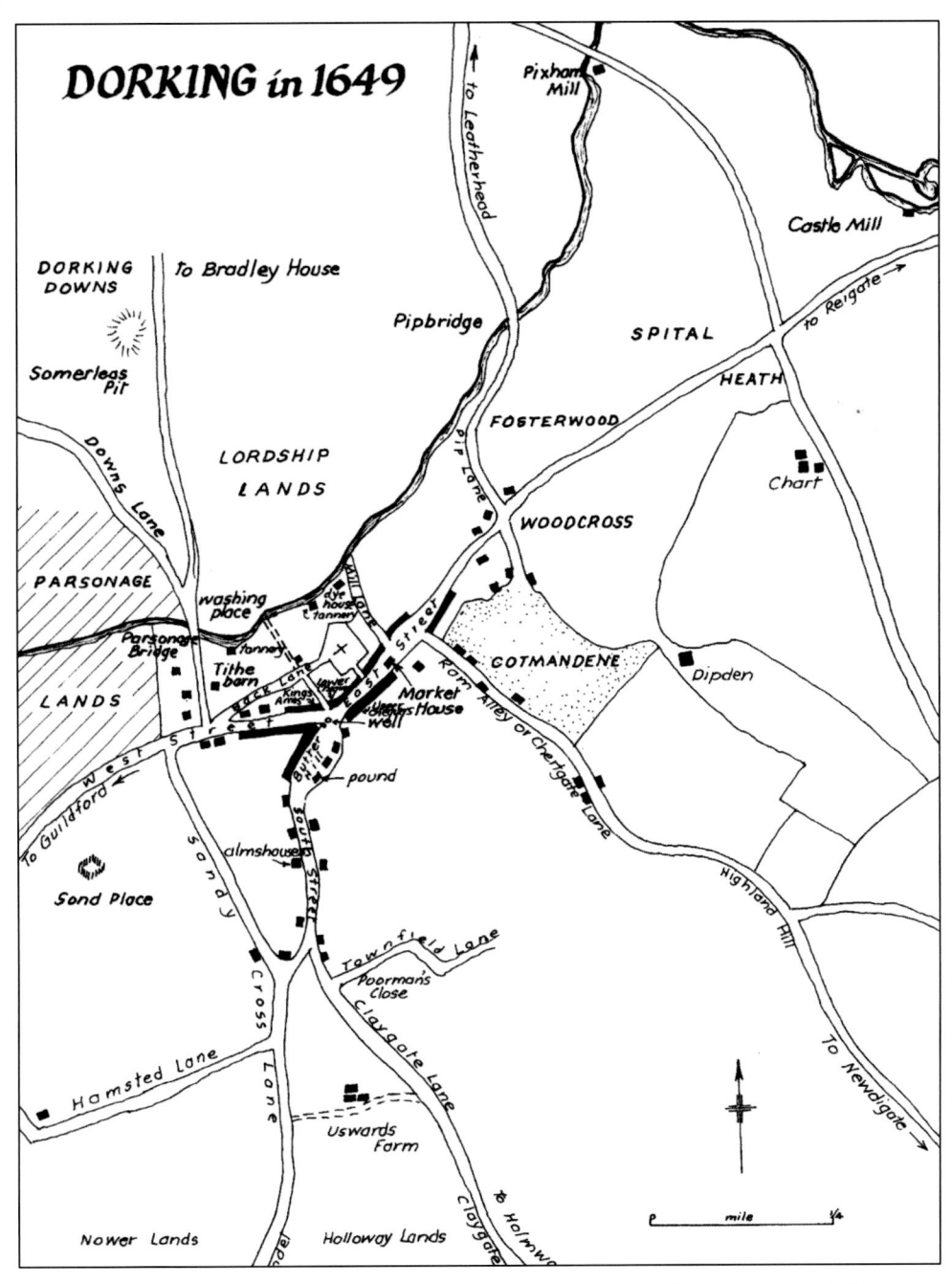

The earliest known map of Dorking dates from 1649, 30 years after Browne and the Mullins family sailed on the *Mayflower*. It gives a good indication of what the town was like in 1620 as the pace of development was slow in the period. This map, drawn from a tracing of the original held at Arundel Castle archives, shows that Dorking had numerous inns, notably Mullins' neighbour, the King's (later Queen's) Arms on the corner of West Street. (Drawing by Beryl Higgins)

The weaver, the shoemaker and the mother of a nation

The market hall which stood on the High Street (then known as East Street) in Dorking until the early 19th century. It had been built in the 1590s. Grain from surrounding farms was traded here and the town gaol was on the upper floor. (Painting by P Daws, from the collection of Dorking Museum)

During the time that Mullins and Browne knew it, the street layout of 'Darking' (as the town's name tended to be spelled in the 17th century) was much as it is now. The long high street, then known as East Street, forked at Pump Corner to become South Street and West Street, the former running south towards Holmwood (the manor's large common grazing land) and the latter being the main road west along the foot of the North Downs. North Street ran down to Back Lane (now Church Street). The only other lanes to speak of were Mill Lane, leading to the mill on the Pipp brook (then known as the Dorking or North brook) which flowed into the River Mole, and Chergate, also known as Ram Alley.

With a population of about 1,400, Dorking was the market town for the surrounding villages and farms and was famous for its poultry,

The weaver, the shoemaker and the mother of a nation

Pump Corner and West Street with the inn known variously as the Queen's or King's Arms, depending on the monarch, in the foreground and Mullins' House in the centre background. The street was painted in the mid-19th century by John Beckett (1799-1864). The inn no longer exists but the name lives on in another building on West Street. (From the collection of Dorking Museum)

especially geese and capons. There were many permanent shops in the town and a market was held twice a week, on Mondays and Thursdays. A gabled, brick-built market house stood on East Street, rather similar to the one that survives in Reigate. There was also a fair held on Ascension Day (in May) which was well known for the sale of lambs. Pump Corner and the top of West Street, where the Mullins family lived, was a busy trading area full of artisans' workshops and the shops of smiths, skinners, weavers, tailors, leather workers, bakers, brewers and butchers.

Not least because beer was a safer drink than water, it is likely that Mullins frequented some of the many inns that surrounded his property:

- the King's Arms at the top of West Street (now HSBC bank)
- the Cardinal's Hat on the southern side of East Street
- The George Inn opposite it (now the Lemon Tree)
- the Upper Chequers (on the site of Robert Dyas)
- the Lower Chequers (later known as the King's Head) on the corner of East Street and North Street (although this may have been built slightly after Mullins' time).

Several of these buildings have survived into the 21st century, although their surrounding barns, gardens and stables have gone.

During the 17th century, buildings in the town were usually timber-framed. Because the steep slopes of the chalk downs to the north and the rutted clays to the south made transportation both difficult and expensive, trees were felled locally rather than timber being brought in from outside the area. Oak was used within a year of felling, before the wood became too hard to work; as a result, many surviving buildings can be accurately dated to within a year of construction by analysis of their tree rings. Some of the domestic and other properties known to the Mullins and Browne families that still survive include:

- Leslie Cottage on Church Street, a timber-framed, two-bay central chimney house built in the 1560s;
- Pear Tree Cottage on Dene Street, a late 16th or early 17th century timber-framed, lobby entrance house;
- The building that now houses the Bourneside Gallery in North Street (formerly the Gun Inn), which formed part of the King's Arms in Mullins' time;
- Parts of the White Horse on the High Street, which date back to the 15th century, though Mullins would not recognise the 18th century exterior, nor that of the re-modelled Dutch House, dating from 1585, which now forms part of the White Horse;
- Parts of what is now the King's Arms on West Street, which date back to the 14th century, although Mullins would probably have known it as a row of cottages;
- The Old House on West Street which has 16th century features; and
- the old Rose and Crown building (now part of Christique), again on West Street, which was a house known as Godfreys in Mullins' time.

The weaver, the shoemaker and the mother of a nation

The property later known as the Gun Inn on North Street, just around the corner from the Mullins' family home. No longer an inn, parts of the timber-framed building survive, with an over-hanging (jettied) first floor. The initials of the 17th century landlord of the King's Arms next door (of which this building is thought to have formed a part), Edward Goodwin, can still be seen on the supports for the window below the gable to the rear. (Drawing by AC Fare from the collection of Dorking Museum.)

Late 16th century trade tokens inscribed 'Edward Goodwin, of Darking in Surry' which would have been in use during the period of Mullins' ownership of the property on West Street.

Goodwin made his living as a chandler (a maker or supplier of candles) and this trade token shows a man making candles. Goodwin was the younger son of the owner of the Queen's Arms on the corner of West Street and North Street, just a few steps east of Mullins' house, and he inherited the inn in 1602. (From the collection of Dorking Museum)

The weaver, the shoemaker and the mother of a nation

Leslie Cottage, Church Street. This timber-framed two-bay house was probably built in the 1560s. It sits on what would have been the track down to the communal washing place. When he was building the house, glover Edward Chitty was fined by the manorial court for muddying the waters of the stream by digging clay for bricks for its base, contaminating the water for those using it downstream. (Image Royston Williamson)

Pear Tree Cottage in Dene Street is a timber-framed lobby entrance house built in the late 16th or early 17th century. (Image Royston Williamson)

Many of these commercial properties would have had cellars for storing perishables at constant temperatures, though the extensive underground diggings that form the famous South Street Caves and other tunnel systems were not excavated until somewhat later.

There was no manor house in Dorking as the lordship of the manor was split between several families. The manorial court met regularly, however, and all men and male youths were required to attend so that the manor's business could be discussed and agreed with the Lord's agent and its rules and regulations enforced, with fines for those in breach. One of the first things that the Pilgrim settlers did on arrival in the new colony was to set up a similar local administrative and judicial system to that of an English manor. For administrative purposes Dorking manor, which stretched as far as the village of Capel in the south, was divided into six tithings, known as 'boroughs': Chipping Borough, East Borough, Milton, Westcote, Holmwood (previously Forreyn Borough) and Waldeborough to the south. Each had an elected official who was responsible for policing crime and behaviour in his tithing. Historically known as the 'headborough', he could also be known as a 'tithingman'; we know that William Mullins fulfilled this role at least once.

The King's Arms, West Street. Dating from the 14th century, this is probably the oldest building in Dorking. Oak-framed, during Mullins' time it was a row of cottages known as Groves after a local fuller. (Image Royston Williamson)

St Martin's parish church served most of the manor's worshippers; to the south a chapel at Capel had been given parish status in the 14th century. Probably built in the 12th century, St Martin's dominated the town. The stone building looked very different to the modern church, with a squat tower instead of a steeple and a number of small extensions off the nave. The vicar in Mullins' youth in the 1570s was Stephen Richman, who had been charged with nonconformity; by the time Mullins bought the West Street property the position was held by John Crayford, who received the living in 1611 from Lord Howard of Effingham. In 1620, there were ten marriages, 65 baptisms and 31 burials in Dorking parish.

We can only speculate about the religious convictions of the Mullins and Browne families. Even if they had been 'Puritan' in outlook, they would not necessarily have felt under threat in the early years of the 17th century (unlike Roman Catholics during the reign of Queen Elizabeth (1558-1603) or Protestants in the reign of Queen Mary (1553-1558) in the previous century). The divide between nonconformists and the English church was not as wide as that between Roman Catholic and Protestant. The English church at this point was Calvinist in doctrine, which meant that the views of the majority of Anglicans and nonconformists were very close. Indeed, since the Gunpowder Plot of 1605, both had been united in their suspicion of Roman Catholicism as the real religious and political threat. However, the English Church continued to use the Prayer Book (based on the Roman Catholic missal); it also tolerated a certain amount of ceremonial as a way of bringing the less educated to God and still retained a hierarchy of bishops and archbishops. Radical nonconformists objected to these elements: they wanted to further reform the Church of England, 'purifying' it of all Roman Catholic practices (hence the term 'Puritan'). They refused to submit to any kind of religious authority that interceded between the individual and God and they opposed the use of sacramental rites and ceremonies in church. King James (who reigned from 1603 to 1625) was far more Calvinist in his personal beliefs than his predecessor, Queen Elizabeth, but he was also hostile to 'Puritans', perhaps due to his upbringing amongst dour Scottish Presbyterians.

In such a relatively tolerant religious climate, why did some nonconformists feel they had to leave England, first for the Netherlands and then for the New World? There had been few prosecutions for non-conformity in the years before the 1620s and the penalties were not as

St Martin's Church, Dorking by John Beckett (1799-1864). A church had existed on the site of St Martin's since before Domesday. The 'medieval' church depicted here was probably built in the 12th century and Mullins would have known it as it was the only church in Dorking. It survived until 1837. (From the collection of Dorking Museum)

severe as during the reigns of Queen Mary and Queen Elizabeth. Those who left tended to belong to extremist 'Separatist' sects which completely rejected any church structure. They were also responding to political events.

The court of King James was notoriously decadent and profligate. It was also beset by a number of scandals. Between 1613 and 1615, the case of Robert Carr and Lady Essex shocked the nation, involving divorce, the poisoning of Sir Thomas Overbury and a dubious pardon (imputed to blackmail of the king over his sexual orientation). In 1614, the 'Addled' Parliament was dissolved after only eight weeks, having failed to grant the king monies he had required: James went on to reign without convening Parliament for seven years. In 1618, it was mooted that a marriage might be arranged between the daughter of the King of Spain and Prince Charles (later Charles I). The plan came to nothing but it revived fears of a tolerance for Roman Catholicism. Such developments led some devout Puritans to conclude that England was no longer a country where the 'godly' could consent to live.

Was William Mullins one of them? It seems likely that at the very least he had sympathy for their thinking. There seems to have been an informal Puritan network operating within England that was sensitive to religious policy emanating from the court of James I and during the time that he was living in West Street, Mullins was called before the Privy Council, a powerful body of advisors to the King. We do not know why he was summoned but, in May 1616, he was held in custody for a short time. He was called for trial again in March 1619 at the Surrey Assizes in Croydon (though his case never went to trial). Once again we do not know why. It is possible that his brushes with the law were for religious offences. If they were, it might explain his sympathy with the Separatists who initiated the voyage of the *Mayflower* and his decision to leave the town of his birth. But religious convictions might not have been the main driver of his decision to leave England: economic factors may have been as important to a shoemaker (and, indeed, to a weaver). A terrible harvest in 1590 had led to famine during his youth. A period of rapid price rises was followed by a period of deep depression and widespread unemployment, particularly in the cloth industry. On the other hand, international trade was increasing, credit was becoming more widely available and a successful colony in the New World would offer a unique business opportunity. A businessman like Mullins and an artisan like Browne may have been responding to both positive and negative economic pressures when they decided to try their luck in the colony of Virginia.

In May 1619, William Mullins sold his Dorking property to glover Ephraim Bothell for £280[1]. Soon afterwards both he and Peter Browne invested in the joint-stock company that would fund the voyage of the *Mayflower*.

---

[1] Caleb Johnson suggests £180 but our researcher checked the original document and £280 seems to be correct. The '2' is blotted, hence the confusion.

The weaver, the shoemaker and the mother of a nation

Above: The former Wheatsheaf Inn on the High Street, a mid-16th century timber-framed building with a cock-fighting pit in its basement, seen here decorated for the coronation of King Edward VII in 1902.

Right: The old Rose and Crown Inn on West Street in the late 19th century. Parts of the interior, contemporary with the Mullins family's time in Dorking, still survive. (Painting by George Gardiner. From the collection of Dorking Museum)

The weaver, the shoemaker and the mother of a nation

Design from a Wedgwood flagon produced to celebrate the 350th anniversary of the sailing of the *Mayflower*. Members of the Wedgwood family have made their home in the Dorking and Leith Hill area since the early 19th century. (From the collection of Dorking Museum. Image by Royston Williamson)

A New Found Land

In 1620, a group of English exiles was living in Leiden, Holland. Many originated in the village of Scrooby in Lincolnshire. Led by William Brewster and his assistant William Bradford, they had rejected the authority of the Protestant church in England and all forms of organised worship. Instead, they took their authority from the Bible, the word of God unmediated by priest or preacher. Having been fined or imprisoned for not attending church services, they had left England in 1608 but were tired of living in exile. These Separatists were looking for a home, a new 'England' where they would be free to live and to worship according to their beliefs and without fear of harassment. They were seeking to establish God's colony on earth. The auspices for a settlement in the New World, however, were not good.

The *Mayflower* expedition was not the first attempt at settlement in the north of the Americas. Nor was it the first by English colonists. Since its discovery by Columbus in 1492, European rulers had laid claim to the continent's riches with scant regard to the rights of its native inhabitants. Spain, Portugal and France had moved quickly to establish a presence in the New World. By 1600, following the conquest of the Aztec and Inca empires, the Spanish had established a vast empire in central and south America and French settlers had made incursions to the north. England had been slow to grasp the opportunities of the New World and did not attempt to establish a colony there until the 1580s when Sir Walter Raleigh (c1582-1618) sponsored a settlement at Roanoke.

Queen Elizabeth had granted Raleigh a charter to

The American Pilgrim Museum in Leiden, the Netherlands, where many of the *Mayflower* party had been living prior to sailing. (Image reproduced by permission of HerenId)

colonise an area in what is now North Carolina, from which his ships might menace Spanish fleets bringing the wealth of South America across the Atlantic. The enterprise was a disaster. Lacking supplies and having got off on a bad footing with the local inhabitants, most of the original settlers elected to return to England after a year. A passing ship, captained by Sir Francis Drake (c1540-1596), took the desperate settlers home, leaving a small garrison at Roanoke. By the time a supply ship arrived with another contingent of colonists bound for Chesapeake Bay in 1587, every man had disappeared without trace. The new colonists were nonetheless deposited to take over the Roanoke settlement, despite the colony's bad relations with local tribes. One hundred and fifteen people were left there, including Virginia Dare, the first English child to be born in the Americas. As England was at war with Spain, it was three years before an English ship was able to return to the colony. When a ship docked in August 1590, all 115 men, women and children had disappeared. What happened to them remains a mystery.

There had been another attempt to establish a colony, at what is now Jamestown in Virginia, just a few years prior to the voyage of the *Mayflower*. The area had been claimed for the English crown during the reign of Queen Elizabeth and named after the Virgin Queen. Now her successor, King James, wished to encourage settlement: a populated colony would pay taxes to the crown and send supplies of goods and raw materials back across the Atlantic.

The expedition of 1607 was funded by the city merchants of the Virginia Company. Again, the settlers fared badly, arriving at a time of drought and too late in the season to plant food crops. Most of the original colonists died before a relief ship carrying supplies and more colonists arrived; others defected to local native American tribes and the colony was threatened by the Spanish. When a supply ship failed to arrive in 1610, the colonists starved. Only sixty of the original 214 settlers survived and they may have done so by turning to cannibalism. Declaring the colony unviable, the settlers had taken the decision to return to England when a relief fleet arrived, bringing the provisions necessary to enable them to remain. Even so, the colony struggled to make a return on the Company's investment and, in 1622, as the *Mayflower* settlers were trying to survive in New England, the local Powhatan people massacred the Jamestown colonists.

'Saints' and 'Strangers'

Despite this sorry history (and with the Jamestown disaster still unfolding as they made their preparations), the Leiden congregation of Separatists determined to settle in the New World. Two of them, John Carver and Robert Cushman, travelled to London to obtain permission to establish themselves in Virginia. In February 1620, a licence to settle was issued to the 'Saints', as the group became known. (They were never known as 'Pilgrims' or 'Pilgrim Fathers' in their own lifetimes; the term came into use in the 1790s.) The Leiden congregation agreed to recognise the authority of the King of England in matters of church and state; in return they received some assurance that they would be allowed to practice their own beliefs unmolested.

The congregation needed to raise sufficient funds to charter a ship, to provision it for the journey, to pay the crew and to equip themselves with the supplies, tools and equipment needed to establish a settlement. With insufficient personal funds to pay for such an undertaking, they turned for finance to a merchant from Staffordshire named Thomas Weston, who had previously got himself into trouble importing seditious religious material into England. He brought together a group of financiers and merchants who became known as the Merchant Adventurers. We do not know if these men were sympathetic to the Separatists' religious cause or whether they were simply investors in search of profits; either way, they agreed to finance the journey and to recruit more settlers as there were insufficient members of the Leiden congregation to make the prospect viable. Under the deal reached with their funders, the settlers would each take a share in the company so that they all had a financial interest in it. They would repay all the expenses of the journey with interest and for seven years their funders would be entitled to all the profits that were expected to come from shipping furs, fish and timber back to England. After that period (assuming the initial debt was paid), the company would be wound up, the profits would be distributed amongst all the shareholders and the colonists would be free of obligation to their funders.

To make up the numbers, seventy or more travellers were recruited, each paying £10 a head to join the expedition. These paying passengers became known as the 'Strangers'. William Mullins and Peter Browne were amongst those who invested and paid to travel (though they may also have been Separatist in their beliefs). Those who invested in the venture were entitled to shares in the company; we know that William Mullins took nine shares in the stock of the Merchant Adventurers. We do not know how he heard of the opportunity or if he was acquainted with anyone involved but he was not alone in looking to establish a business in the new colony.

The agreement between the funders and the Leiden congregation sets out how the colony was to operate. The Separatists wished to establish a settlement driven by the word of God rather than by the demands of commerce. They resisted attempts to impose a long working week (which would maximise profits for their investors) as longer working hours would have reduced the time available for worship. This led to tension between the Separatists and those who were funding the enterprise and were keen to see a healthy return. With an investment to protect, Mullins and Browne would have taken a keen interest in these deliberations.

Commemorative plate depicting William Mullins, the shoemaker. (From the collection of Dorking Museum)

The Mayflower – 'meat for fishes'

The ship that would take the travellers across the Atlantic was chartered in Rotherhithe, Kent. No details of her design or dimensions survive but the *Mayflower* was probably only some 27 metres feet (88 feet) long and weighed in the region of 180 tons. A small, ageing ship with three masts, she had been part-owned by her captain, Christopher Jones, since 1608. She had nearly been lost when blown 300 miles off course on a voyage to Norway and between 1610 and 1620 she had plied the wine trade between England and La Rochelle in France. In the spring of 1620, wines from Bordeaux were being unloaded in Rotherhithe when Captain Jones was approached by Robert Cushman and Thomas Weston. The *Mayflower* had never crossed the Atlantic; indeed, her longest voyage had been to Malaga in Spain. Nor had her captain ever crossed the ocean. Wisely, he engaged two ship's mates who had previously made the crossing to Virginia and who were familiar with the perils of its coastline.

The *Mayflower* at sea by Allen Stanley Pollack, 1949. (Susannah Horne)

The 'Strangers' were the first to board. William Mullins, who was now nearing fifty years old, his wife Alice, seven-year-old Joseph and his teenage sister, Priscilla, were amongst those who joined the ship at Rotherhithe in July 1620. Each family was allotted space for one and a half tons of goods. As well as personal possessions, Mullins took with him 21 dozen (252 pairs) of shoes and thirteen pairs of boots, an indication of his intent to set up in business once the colony was established. Accompanying them was a manservant, Robert Carter, who is also thought to have been from Dorking.

In mid-July, the *Mayflower* sailed from Rotherhithe to Southampton. The Leiden Separatists sailed from Delfthaven to rendezvous with the rest of the party there. It was intended that their ship, the *Speedwell*, would cross the Atlantic with the *Mayflower*. With them was a soldier, Captain Myles Standish, and his wife Rose. He was to act as the colony's 'protection' officer against whatever dangers it should encounter. At Southampton the settlers, none of whom were experienced seamen, recruited six young men to teach them how to use the inshore boat that the *Mayflower* carried and which would be left with the colonists to enable them to fish and navigate coastal waters. They also recruited a young cooper named John Alden to maintain and repair the colony's casks and barrels. This was a vital role as the barrels contained food and their only supplies of fresh water. Both Standish and Alden were to play a part in the Mullins story.

The group planned to leave England in late July 1620 but preparations did not go smoothly. Provisions for the journey, as well as farming supplies and equipment, had to be procured and split between the two ships. Wrangling over money caused delay and some stores had to be sold to pay port duties, leading to concerns about a shortfall in provisions. The ships finally sailed on August 5th, only a little later than planned. On board were a mixed bag of hardened seamen, merchant adventurers and devout Pilgrims. There were far more men than women: a number of single men travelled alone, many households brought one or more male servants with them and many family men travelled ahead of their families, taking older sons with them but leaving wives, daughters and youngers sons to travel later when the colony was established. Amongst the party were also four young children who had been removed from their mother (on the grounds of her adultery) and sent to the New World in the company of the Separatists so that there should be no question of them inheriting family money. Only one of these children survived the first winter.

The *Speedwell* did not make it further than the English Channel before beginning to leak. Already behind schedule, the small convoy put into the port of Dartmouth for repairs before setting sail again. However, the ship's crew had no faith in the vessel's chances of crossing nearly 3,000 miles of ocean. On September 1st the *Speedwell*, accompanied by the *Mayflower*, put in to Plymouth for further repairs. All the time that the ships remained in port, vital provisions for the journey were being depleted. Concern grew that if they delayed any longer the party would arrive in Virginia too late to establish themselves on land before winter set in. Robert Cushman wrote to a friend that the *Speedwell* was *'as leaky as a sieve'*; he was convinced that had she stayed more than a few hours more at sea she would have sunk. He calculated that if the colonists remained in port, eating their provisions, they would arrive in the colony with no more than a month's worth of supplies. Despairing of ever setting sail and less than impressed with the captain's attitude towards his passengers, Cushman told his correspondent that he expected to become *'meat for fishes'*.

It was reluctantly accepted that the *Speedwell* was unseaworthy. She was overladen, had been refitted to carry more canvas than her timbers would bear and was incapable of crossing the ocean. The expedition had to be reduced to one ship but the *Mayflower* could not accommodate all the travellers and their provisions. Some twenty colonists, perhaps the most perspicacious amongst them (including Cushman), elected to stay behind with a large quantity of provisions. The rest were crammed aboard the *Mayflower*. Over 100 people, a quarter of them children, plus three pregnant women, occupied the gun deck. (The ship needed to be armed with cannon, which would have been fired from the gun ports had the ship come under attack from pirates or shipping hostile to English interests.) The settlers' food stores and other supplies, personal possessions and equipment were held in the cargo deck below: clothing, shoes, bedding, light armour, hunting weapons, household cooking pots and agricultural and construction tools. The ship also carried dogs, goats and poultry. Crewed by between thirty and forty men, the *Mayflower* left Plymouth on 16th September 1620.

The *Mayflower* approaching land. (Engraving by John A Lowell, 1905. Library of Congress)

The passengers had already been aboard for weeks. The voyage was predicted to take six gruelling weeks; in fact, it took eight. The ship hit autumnal westerly winds, increasing the voyage time. Conditions on board were cramped, damp and insanitary; there were no toilet facilities and passengers dared not venture on deck often for fear of getting in the way of the crew or being swept overboard in rough seas. They had little privacy, over 100 people being confined to a space 17 metres (55 feet) by 7 metres (23 feet) with only flimsy home-made partitioning. The ship was buffeted by gales and the timbers leaked. Passengers were unable to keep dry; they suffered prolonged sea-sickness (particularly the women and children who were confined to safety below decks) and had insufficient food. Many fell seriously ill. It is surprising, given the extent of their suffering, that the party lost only one passenger and one crew member on the voyage, though they gained two babies. Born on board, they revelled in the names of Oceanus and Peregrine (Pilgrim).

By the time the group arrived in the Americas, the *Mayflower* had a collapsed main beam and the travellers were malnourished, weak and hardly in a fit condition to begin the hard physical labour of establishing a settlement.

The *Mayflower* in Plymouth harbour by William Halsall, 1882. (From the collection of Pilgrim Hall Museum, Plymouth, Massachusetts.)

The Mayflower Compact

Land was spotted on November 9th and the party made landfall the following day at Cape Cod in what is now Massachusetts. This was a long way north of their destination in Virginia. When attempts to sail south failed, the party decided to establish themselves where they were. Unfortunately, they had no legal right of settlement in Cape Cod, a situation that they would later have to regularise by applying for a patent. (It was granted the following year.)

In the meantime, the colonists drew up a contract between themselves setting out what they were going to do and how they were going to govern themselves, probably in response to early disagreements and questioning of the authority of their leaders. It was the first political document drawn up in what was to become New England and became known as the Mayflower Compact. Dated 11th November 1620 and probably read out to the company (as many would have been unable to read), the agreement set out that all were loyal subjects of King James who had set out to establish a colony in Virginia

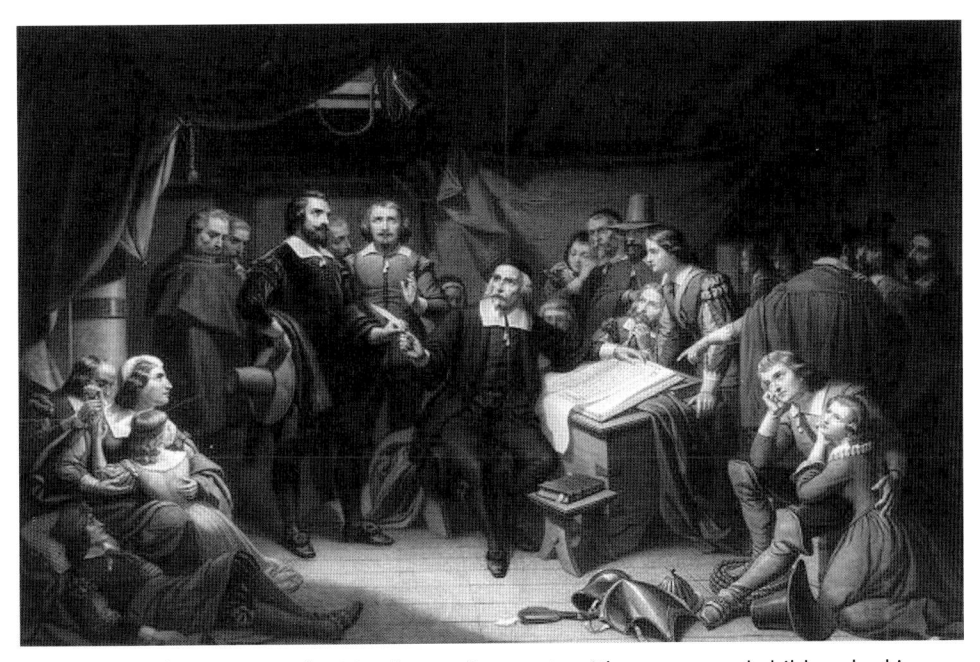

The male Pilgrims write the Mayflower Compact, with women and children looking on. (1859 engraving by Gauthier after a painting by TH Matteson. Library of Congress)

but that they now covenanted to bind themselves together into a 'body politic', recognised by each of them, in order to facilitate their survival and to establish an orderly settlement. The agreement allowed them to make whatever laws were considered necessary and to put in place whatever administrative and judicial systems were required for the good of the colony. It was, of course, the male settlers who drew up the Compact and it would be the male settlers to whom these powers were granted. The names added to the Compact were later recorded from the original by William Bradford in his journal. William Mullins' name was amongst them, as was Peter Browne's; the name of Mullins' manservant, Robert Carter, was not. This suggests that Carter was under 21 when the Compact was drawn up and therefore legally a minor. Like Mullins' wife and children, he had no independent status in law.

The Mayflower Compact

IN THE NAME OF GOD, AMEN. We, whose names are underwritten, the Loyal Subjects of our dread Sovereign Lord King *James*, by the Grace of God, of *Great Britain, France* and *Ireland*, King, *Defender of the Faith*, &c. Having undertaken for the Glory of God, the Advancement of the Christian Faith, and the Honour of our King and Country, a Voyage to plant the first Colony in the northern parts of *Virginia*: Do by these Presents, solemnly and mutually, in the Presence of God and one another, covenant and combine ourselves together into a civil Body Politick, for our better Ordering and Preservation, and constitute, and frame, such just and equal Laws, Ordinances, Acts, Constitutions, and Offices from time to time, as shall be thought most meet and convenient for the general Good of the Colony; unto which we promise all due Submission and Obedience. IN WITNESS whereof we have hereunto subscribed our names at *Cape Cod* the eleventh of *November*, In the Reign of our Sovereign Lord King *James* of *England, France*, and *Ireland* the eighteenth, and of *Scotland*, the fifty-fourth, *Anno Domini*, 1620

The names of the following (male) travellers were recorded from the original Compact by William Bradford in his journal:

John Carver – the first governor of the colony
William Bradford – the colony's second governor
Edward Winslow
William Brewster – the colony's religious leader
Isaac Allerton
Myles Standish – the colony's protection officer
John Alden – the ship's cooper
John Turner
Francis Eaton
James Chilton
John Craxton
John Billington
Moses Fletcher
John Goodman
Samuel Fuller
Christopher Martin
William Mullins
William White
Richard Warren
John Howland
Stephen Hopkins
Digery Priest
Thomas Williams
Gilbert Winslow
Edmund Margesson
Peter Browne
Richard Bitteridge
George Soule
Edward Tilly
John Tilly
Francis Cooke
Thomas Rogers
Thomas Tinker
John Ridgdale
Edward Fuller
Richard Clarke
Richard Gardiner
John Allerton
Thomas English
Edward Doten
Edward Leister

The weaver, the shoemaker and the mother of a nation

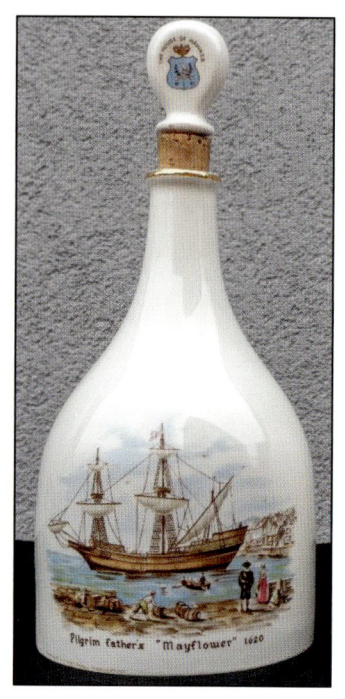

Left: Wedgwood flagon produced to celebrate the 350th anniversary of the sailing of the *Mayflower*. (From the collection of Dorking Museum. Image by Royston Williamson)

Below: Model of the *Mayflower* by David Crump. No plans or descriptions of the ship survive so all reconstructions are speculative. (From the collection of Dorking Museum. Image by Royston Williamson.)

'An unknown coast'

The first party went ashore on the day the Compact was signed but they found the initial landing place, in the Cape Cod area, unsuitable as an anchorage and base. Winter conditions were not conducive to exploration. *'And for the season it was winter, and they that know the winters of that country know them to be sharp and violent and subject to cruel and fierce storms, dangerous to travel to known places, much more to search an unknown coast'*, recalled William Bradford later. During November, their fishing boat made several expeditions along the coastline. On one they found stores of corn buried by native Americans for use the next season which they took back to the ship. By early December, the weather was very cold and one of those involved recalled that *'the water froze on our clothes, and made them many times like coats of iron'*. They came across a burial place and dug up some graves, hoping to find more corn. Overnighting on land they were attacked by members of the Nauset people, who had had run-ins in the past with French traders taking members of the tribe into slavery and selling them in Spain. Forced to move on, they rounded the cape into what would become known as Plymouth Harbor. They had been in the colony for nearly two months looking for a place to settle and winter was now well advanced. The place where they found themselves was the best of any they had seen and they elected to establish their settlement there.

The area had been the home of native peoples from as early as 12,000-9,000BC. When the settlers arrived it was inhabited by the Wampanoag people; they called the area Mattakeesett *'place of many fish'*, from which the name Massachusetts derives. King James may have granted rights of settlement but this was without the knowledge or consent of those who already occupied the land. The settlers were aware of the presence of native peoples; they had stolen their corn stores and dug up their graves. Nor were the local inhabitants isolated and ignorant of Europe. A hundred years of exploration and trade had brought the indigenous peoples of North America into regular contact with Europeans. By 1620, English fleets had been fishing off what would become known as New England for 120 years and sometimes fishermen would come ashore to resupply, to rest or sometimes to over-winter. Whaling expeditions also plied the coast and put ashore.

The weaver, the shoemaker and the mother of a nation

The territory may not have been settled by Europeans but it was not unknown; it had been mapped and its bays and rivers had been renamed. Some of the local people had had contact with passing traders; some had even picked up a smattering of the English language.

Desperate as they must have been to leave their cramped and squalid conditions, the settlers had arrived too late in the year to establish dwellings on land; most of them would have to live aboard ship until the spring when the *Mayflower* returned to England. Winter was far colder than the English settlers were used to and, after their gruelling sea voyage, many were in a weakened condition. It was the end of December by the time they began taking supplies ashore. Building began in early January, an inauspicious month given the northerly latitude in which New Plymouth was located. At this point, Peter Browne went missing. On 12th January he and three other men

The landing of the Pilgrims at Plymouth, December 1620. This mid-19th century lithograph shows the male Pilgrims coming ashore for the first time at the place that they would name Plymouth, overseen by a native American who is rather inadequately clothed for the severe New England winter! (N. Currier. Library of Congress)

went into the woods to cut roofing thatch. Following their dogs further into the wilderness in pursuit of a deer, he and John Goodman became disorientated and hopelessly lost. Inadequately dressed and with no food, the two spent a freezing night in the trees, in fear of mountain lions. They survived but when they finally found their way back to the harbour, they were suffering from frostbite.

The effort of building the first settlement and finding the means to survive winter with little food took an immediate toll. By January, large numbers of settlers had fallen sick with a combination of scurvy (for they had been unable to grow fruit or vegetables), pneumonia and malnourishment. With no hope of re-supply or outside assistance, one by one the settlers died. Seventeen succumbed in February 1621 alone. Amongst them was William White, whose wife had given birth to a son on board the *Mayflower*. On 21st February, William Mullins died. He had been in the colony just over three months.

The landing of the Pilgrims on 22nd December 1620. This American engraving depicts the Pilgrims coming ashore after over a month trying to find a suitable place to settle. They are observed by a native American to whom they pay no attention. Women, children and the sick are depicted as being carried ashore. In fact they continued to live aboard the ship until the spring (Library of Congress)

Mullins composed his will on the day of his death. It is thought to have been the first will written in the colony: unlike many of the travellers, Mullins had substantial assets to distribute, both in the colony and in England. The will was probably dictated to John Carver, the colony's governor, and was witnessed by the *Mayflower's* surgeon, Dr Giles Heale, and its captain, Christopher Jones. Mullins left £10 each to his wife, to his children Joseph and Priscilla, who had accompanied him to the colony, and to his eldest son, William, who had remained in England. To his eldest daughter (Sarah), who had also remained in England, he left 10 shillings. Sarah was already married and Mullins left her comparatively little in his will compared with her siblings. This does not necessarily mean that relations between them were strained; presumably, he believed her to be well provided for already. He also left William all the stock, bonds and debts owed to him in England, and his share of land in the colony, should William wish to join his siblings in the New World. The rest of his stock in Virginia (as he still called it) was to be shared between his wife, Joseph and Priscilla. He requested that his stock of shoes and boots be sold to the Company for £40. His nine shares in the Company were distributed between his wife and children.

Resin model of William Mullins, the shoemaker. (From the collection of Dorking Museum)

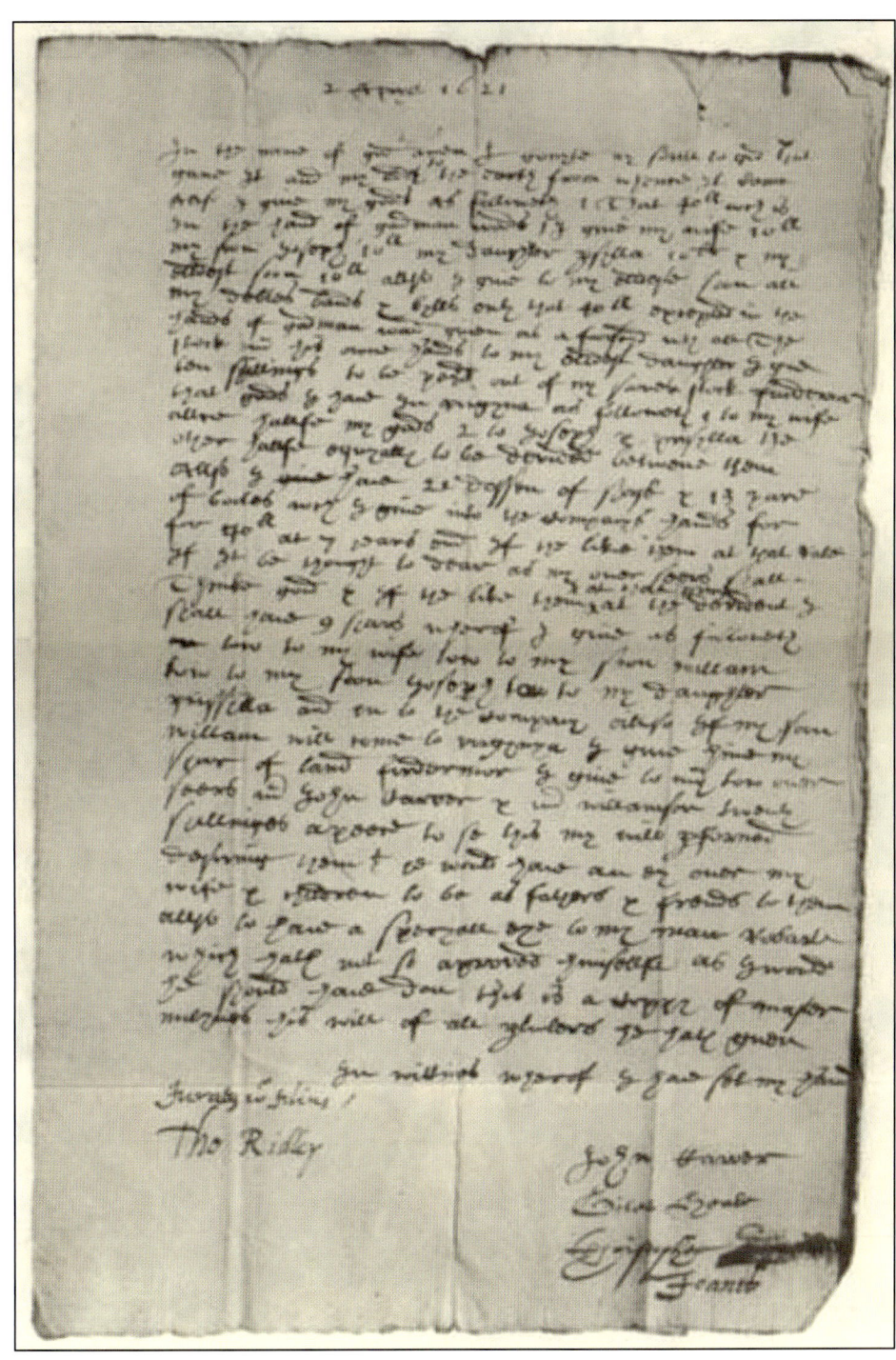

The weaver, the shoemaker and the mother of a nation

Clerk's copy of the will of William Mullins held by the Prerogative Court of Canterbury. In the document his name is spelled 'Mullens', but spelling was not standardised in this period. His is the only surviving will from one of the passengers who died during the colonists' first winter. (The National Archives PROB 11/138/51. Crown Copyright)

William Mullins died in the knowledge that he was leaving his wife and two children alone in the precarious colony, with just one inadequate manservant to assist and protect them. This he recognised in his request to John Carver and 'Mr Williamson' to have *'an eye'* to his wife and children and to *'be as fathers and friends to them'* and to have a *'special eye'* for Robert Carter, whose service had disappointed him. The other colonists had little opportunity to offer guidance to the young man who had lost his master, however: Carter, too, was dead within months.

The 'Mr Williamson' referred to was probably William Brewster, spiritual leader of the colony. Shortly before leaving Holland, he had established a printing press in Leiden and had been smuggling illegal religious tracts into England. He feared that even in the colony he was at risk of arrest if the authorities in England learned of his whereabouts and Mullins was using Brewster's pseudonym to protect his identity. Mullins' will was carried back to England when the *Mayflower* returned. On 23rd July, probate was issued either to Sarah Blunden, Mullins' married daughter, or to his elder son (the records are contradictory). He was described as *'late of Dorking in the county of Surrey, but deceased in parts beyond the seas'*.

'A hideous and desolate wilderness, full of wild beasts and wild men'

It was a miracle that the *Mayflower* colony escaped the extinction of the Roanoke settlement. Nearly half the *Mayflower's* passengers had died before the winter was out, including Rose Standish, the wife of the colony's protection officer. Of those that remained, few had experience of farming or fishing in their home country, let alone the skills to survive in a strange land. Massachusetts seemed to them a desolate wilderness. *'What could they see but a hideous and desolate wilderness, full of wild beasts and wild men?'* wrote William Bradford, *'And what multitudes there might be of men they knew not.'* In fact, it was a 'wild man' who was to be the settlers' saviour.

The colonists were totally isolated, 500 miles from the nearest settlement at Jamestown. At their back was the savage ocean that they had crossed and before them a vast unknown continent. They also feared attack from native people. It is hard to imagine a group of people so far from comfort and civilisation. With the arrival of spring, they set to establishing their tiny village and communal farming and to clearing land to plant crops. Unfortunately, like the Roanake community (whose members were in the main aristocratic), the Plymouth settlers had little or no farming experience. Those amongst them who described themselves as 'farmers' were farm owners rather than labourers who knew how to work the land and much of what they did know was not relevant to the conditions of the 'wilderness' in which they found themselves. Their occupations were artisanal; amongst them were two tailors, a printer, several merchants, a silk worker, a shopkeeper and a hatter. They had packed sundials, candle snuffers, a drum and trumpet (and Mullins' supplies of shoes and boots), and some fishing equipment, but they had no horse or plough. Nor were they experienced in hunting, which was an aristocratic sport in England rather than a means of making a living. Even their protector seemed unsuited to the role, being so small in stature that he was known as 'Captain Shrympe'. They were reliant on their faith.

As they built their dwellings, their supplies dwindled to the point where they were virtually starving. It was doubtful that the colonists would survive long enough to bring in their first harvest. Ironically, they were surrounded by edible riches. Had they known how to catch, harvest or cultivate the fruits of the land and sea their future would have been secure; as it was, they faced a bleak prospect. Suddenly, as William Bradford put it, *'there presented himself a savage which caused alarm. He very boldly came all alone and along the houses straight to the rendezvous, where we intercepted him, not suffering him to go in, as undoubtedly he would, out of his boldness. He saluted us in English and bade us 'welcome'.'* The colonists had travelled 3,000 miles to a spot quite remote from the land that they had intended to settle and found an English speaker. They must have been astonished.

The native American was a man named Samoset, who had learned a few words of English from fishermen who had worked the coast. He stayed a night in the settlement and returned with more men to trade. Even more astonishingly, he introduced the settlers to a man named Tisquantum who spoke fluent English. 'Squanto' was to be the saving of the colony. By sheer luck, no doubt interpreted by some as the hand of God, the settlers had found the most fluent English speaker for hundreds (if not thousands) of miles. Even better, he was sympathetic to their plight.

In reality, the fact that the colonists came across an English speaker is not quite as miraculous as it seems, given the number of European ships crossing the Atlantic in the early 17th century. Squanto could probably speak not one but two European languages. Little is known about his early life but it is likely that he was a member of the Wampanoag tribe and that his native language was a form of Algonquian. He had been taken captive and spent more than a decade in Europe, firstly as a slave in Spain, then working for a merchant in London and finally as an interpreter on a whaler. By the time he returned to his native land, his people had been wiped out, probably by smallpox introduced from Europe.

Squanto's ability to translate for him, enabled the colony's governor, (now William Bradford), to agree a mutually beneficial peace treaty between the settlers and the leader of the local Wampanoag people. Squanto settled with the colonists and became their teacher, interpreter, ambassador and friend. He showed them what they could and could not eat, taught them how to plant corn and catch wildfowl, how to fish and how to fertilise the soil with rotting fish. He helped them to establish relations with the local chief, Osamequin (Massasoit), avoiding the misunderstandings and bad relations that had beset the

The weaver, the shoemaker and the mother of a nation

Jamestown colony. Ultimately, he helped them to set up a valuable beaver trade that would bring them the cash to pay off their debts. Beaver pelts were in great demand in Europe and this proved to be the colony's salvation.

All this while, the *Mayflower* had remained, an insurance policy should the settlement fail completely. This meant that the settlers continued to pay the wages of crew and captain, running up more debt for the Company. Finally, in April 1621, Captain Jones sailed for home, bearing William Mullins' will to be proved in England but without the furs, timber and fish that the venture's investors in London were expecting. Though half his crew were dead, Jones reached England in a month. He died three years later and, when the ship was valued for probate purposes, it was described as being *'in ruins'*. The *Mayflower* was very likely broken up shortly afterwards. Despite their depleted numbers, the colonists had elected to remain; in debt to the Company, they had little option.

It is estimated that only 54 colonists were still alive when the ship departed, half of them children. They included the Mullins family, now come ashore and making their home in the colony without husband, father and master. It was not long before William Mullins' wife, young son and manservant followed him to the grave. All are buried in unmarked plots at the Coles Hill Burial Ground, Plymouth. Less than six months after the family's arrival in Massachusetts, the teenage Priscilla Mullins had lost (step) mother, father, brother and servant. She was now an orphan on the new continent, with no male relative to provide her with protection or to undertake the hard physical labour that would be required to establish and maintain a home in the colony.

For the moment, Priscilla became a member of the household of William Brewster, the illicit printer on the run from the authorities. She was under his protection and, no doubt, his supervision. Caleb Johnson's research indicates that the first winter took a particularly hard toll on the women of the colony: 78% of the eighteen adult women who made the crossing died during that season. Priscilla would have found herself in a community of only five adult women (very soon to be four) amongst over fifty men and children. It is telling that Susanna White, whose husband, William, had died on the same day as Priscilla's father, remarried within months of her husband's death. She married Edward Winslow, whose wife had died during that same winter. As the mother of a young son and with a baby born on the voyage, she would have known that she and her children were unlikely to survive if she did not remarry. Similarly, Winslow, with young children in his care, also needed to find them a mother. Priscilla's situation was not as desperate; as a young single woman she was vulnerable but she was also heir to all her father's property, as well as being one of the only marriageable women in the colony. Once Susanna White was married Priscilla was probably the only unattached woman of marriageable age; when it came to marriage she would not lack for choice.

In November 1621, a year after the first party had arrived, the ship *Fortune* arrived in the colony, bringing more single men. She had been dispatched by the Company to bring more settlers, many of them the wives and children of the *Mayflower* party. However, as little to profit the Company had been sent back across the Atlantic on the *Mayflower*, the ship brought little in the way of goods and materials. Amongst the new arrivals was Martha Ford; heavily pregnant, she gave birth the day after her arrival in Plymouth but lost her husband either on the voyage or shortly after arrival. She was left in a far more precarious position in the New World than Priscilla.

A wooden tankard believed to have been the property of Peter Browne is on display at the Pilgrim Hall Museum in Plymouth, Massachusetts. (Image courtesy of the Pilgrim Hall Museum, Plymouth, Massachusetts)

It was in a letter written by Edward Winslow to be carried back across the Atlantic on the returning *Fortune*, that the first description of the colonists' celebration of their survival for which they are so famous appears. Winslow recorded good crops of Indian corn and some barley that autumn, though the peas had shrivelled disappointingly in the sun. After the harvest was gathered in, the governor sent four men to find some wildfowl *'so that we might after a more special manner rejoice together, after we had gathered the fruit of our labors'*. Winslow recorded that the four killed sufficient fowl to feed the colonists for a week and that the local 'Indians' and their 'king' feasted with them for three days, bringing five deer as their contribution to the feast.

It is usually said that the Thanksgiving tradition which is still celebrated in the United States today had its origins in this feast. In reality it is likely to have originated in later ad hoc religious proclamations to give thanks for fortuitous events, but it has become an iconic part of the popular story of the founding of the nation.

A replica of Peter Browne's house in Plimoth Plantation, Massachusetts. (Image reproduced courtesy of Joanne Barnard)

The weaver, the shoemaker and the mother of a nation

'Why don't you speak for yourself, John?'

In 1858, a descendant of Priscilla Mullins, the poet Henry Wadsworth Longfellow (1807-1882), wrote a long poem purporting to tell the tale of the courtship and marriage of the young woman from Dorking. The publication of *'The Courtship of Miles Standish'* took Priscilla from obscurity to national heroine. Longfellow claimed to have based his version of events on family history, passed down from generation to generation and eventually written down in 1814. He presented Priscilla as a lively and self-possessed young woman whom Standish, not long widowed, wishes to marry. Priscilla, however, much preferred the young cooper, John Alden. As Longfellow tells it, John was sent to request Priscilla's hand in marriage on behalf of Standish; when he does so, Priscilla asks him why he does not ask on his own behalf, politely refusing Standish's proposal. Longfellow depicts Standish as furiously departing on a military mission, bringing back the head of an unfortunate Native American as a trophy. Priscilla then fears he might claim her once more before she is married to Alden.

Postcard depicting Priscilla Mullins and her husband, John Alden. The features of both are guesswork as it is unlikely that either ever sat for their portrait. (From a painting by JPG Ferris. Reproduced by permission of the Alden Kindred of America)

Parts of the tale are plausible. Alden and Standish were on good terms and probably shared lodgings; Standish may have trusted Alden to act as his proxy. Priscilla was one of the only unmarried women of child-bearing age in the colony; no doubt there was competition for her affections. (Peggy M Baker has shown that by late 1621 there were probably eighteen marriageable men - bachelors or widowers - in the settlement.) For her part, Priscilla had to consider which man offered the best prospect of survival and prosperity, for herself and for any children she might have. She chose John from amongst a pool of suitors, many of them older, or more experienced and well-connected within the colony, than the young ship's cooper. Other elements are probably nonsense. In the poem, Standish is reported killed by a poisoned arrow, Alden's grief at the loss of his dear betrayed friend finally bringing him and Priscilla together, only for Standish to reappear, alive and well, at the wedding asking forgiveness for his anger and wishing Priscilla well.

So who was John Alden? Little is known of the early life of the ship's cooper. He is thought to have been born in about 1598, so would have been in his early twenties when he left England. He must have been of age (over 21) as he was a signatory to the Mayflower Compact. Possibly from Harwich, and a relative of the ship's captain, he had been employed in Southampton to look after the ship's barrels. When the *Mayflower* returned to England in the spring of 1621, Alden had been given the option of staying with the colonists or returning with the ship. Neither of these were safe options given the dangers of sea voyages in the period and the mounting death toll in the colony. Possibly his feelings for Priscilla were a factor in his decision to stay. Longfellow certainly liked to think so, depicting the

Priscilla and John Alden

John and Priscilla Alden from a postcard, mid-20th century. (Public domain)

colonists waving a tearful farewell to the *Mayflower* as she sets sail for England and Alden, eager to return with her, changing his mind on seeing a dejected Priscilla, and deciding to remain for her sake. *'There is no land so sacred,'* he says, *'no air so pure and wholesome/ as is the air she breathes'*

Alden was made welcome in the colony. Bradford recalled that he was *'a hopeful young man'* and *'much desired'*. Longfellow presents the early years of the colony as idyllic, orderly and aspirational. Alden builds a home for his bride-to-be with latticed windows and oiled paper panes, with a well and an orchard nearby.

> *Ever of her he thought, when he fashioned the walls of his dwelling;*
> *Ever of her he thought, when he delved in the soil of his garden;*
> *Ever of her he thought of her, when he read in his Bible on Sunday*
> *Praise of virtuous woman, as she is described in the Proverbs.*

Priscilla is presented as being industrious and thrifty: she spins wool and returns from her wedding on a white steer, neither of which would have been possible as the colony had neither sheep nor cattle. Longfellow celebrated the simple heroism and hard-working virtues of the colonists. For him, the marriage marks a new beginning, not just for John and Priscilla, or the colonists more generally, but for Mankind:

An illustration from an edition of Longfellow's narrative poem, *The Courtship of Miles Standish* depicts Priscilla Mullins' wedding procession with the bride riding a white ox. (Public domain)

The weaver, the shoemaker and the mother of a nation

> *Meanwhile the bridegroom went forth and stood with the bride at the doorway,*
> *Breathing the perfumed air of that warm and beautiful morning.*
> *Touched with autumnal tints, but lonely and sad in the sunshine,*
> *Lay extended before them the land of toil and deprivation;*
> *There were the graves of the dead, and the barren waste of the sea-shore,*
> *There the familiar fields, the groves of pine, and the meadows;*
> *But to their eyes transfigured, it seemed as the Garden of Eden,*
> *Filled with the presence of God, whose voice was the sound of the ocean.*

The symbolism is clear: John and Priscilla's was not just a national mission but a divine one, to establish a new Eden in a new land.

THE COURTSHIP OF MILES STANDISH
Associated Exhibitors

ALTHOUGH this is based upon Longfellow's poem, the trimmings are from history. There are moments of storm, of mutiny—there is disaster and death. The picture was an ambitious effort, but fell far short. Here is America's oldest triangle, *John Alden* (Charles Ray, of course), *Miles Standish* and *Priscilla Mullins*.

Priscilla Mullins with her suitors from the film version of the Standish/Alden/Mullins story. It is presented here as the oldest American love triangle. Unfortunately, all copies of the film have been lost.

The weaver, the shoemaker and the mother of a nation

The poem caught the imagination of 19th century Americans and was a best seller in Britain too. Reprinted and illustrated many times, it remains popular. Largely due to Longfellow, Alden's courtship of Priscilla Mullins is now the stuff of national myth, celebrated in thousands of paintings, statuettes and postcards. It was even made into a film in 1923. Unfortunately, the movie ruined the career of lead actor Charles Ray.

In practical terms, the marriage of a young, healthy couple, who could be expected to produce a large family, was vital to the long-term viability of the colony. The Alden's first child, Elizabeth, was born in 1623. She was followed by nine siblings.

Poster for the 1923 film of *the Courtship of Myles Standish*. Much is made in the blurb of the two heroic male characters – no mention is made of Priscilla! (Public Domain)

The weaver, the shoemaker and the mother of a nation

Populating the colony

Priscilla and her husband lived alongside the surviving settlers, and those who had joined them later on the *Fortune,* in the small New Plymouth community. Two more ships, the *Anne* and the *Little James*, arrived in 1623, bringing more inhabitants. In that year, the colony's lands were divided up amongst the settlers, with each member being allocated an acre. The document detailing the allotment is damaged and the number of acres allotted to the Aldens cannot be read but it is likely that John Alden was allotted five acres, Priscilla having inherited the entitlements of her father, mother and brother. The Aldens' holding of garden land on the northern side of the town was close to that of Captain Standish.

Peter Browne also received his allotted acre. Shortly afterwards, he married Martha Ford, the widow who had given birth almost immediately on arrival in the colony. She had been allotted four acres (the entitlement for herself, her deceased husband and two children). Peter and Martha established a home for Martha's two young children, John and Martha Ford, and went on to have two children of their own. It is not known if Priscilla remained close to the young man from her home town in England but, interestingly, Browne and his wife named their second daughter, born in 1627, Priscilla. (His first daughter's name was Mary.)

The situation between the settlers and the local people, with whom the original colonists had established good relations, became more complicated when another (very ill-prepared) party arrived to found the new Wessagussett settlement. The Plymouth colony grew in size. More people crossed the ocean, bringing with them cattle and livestock. In 1627, the colony's cattle were divided between various groups of settlers; the Aldens and neighbouring families were allotted a heifer that had come over on the ship *Jacob,* while Peter Browne and his family and neighbours were allotted a red heifer and two goats.

In 1628, after years of wrangling between the investment company and the settlers, a handful of men (John Alden amongst them) bought out the shares of most of the failing company's shareholders. The colonists were no longer obliged to pay all their profits to London (though they were still paying off their loan and interest on it). They were free to acquire more land and to move out of the original settlement. Consequently, the colony spread along the coastline. The Aldens were granted 100 acres to farm across the bay to the north of the original New Plymouth settlement. In about 1629, they built a house; for several years they lived there during the summer but returned to the comforts of New Plymouth during the harsh winters. In 1632, permission was sought from the colony to set up a separate settlement at the site with its own church. Joining them in the new village was John Alden's old rival, Captain Standish, as well as William Brewster, the colony's religious leader, once Priscilla's guardian. The town that was eventually established was named Duxbury, probably after Duxbury Manor, one of the historic Standish estates in Lancashire. It was in Duxbury that the Aldens brought up their children. They lived there for over fifty years and their daughter, Sarah, went on to marry Standish's son Alexander, bringing the families even closer.

Peter Browne married again when his wife, Martha, died in 1630. He fathered another two children but died himself in 1633 during a period of unidentified sickness that spread through the colony, taking the lives of several settlers. An inventory of his estate shows that he owned 130 bushels of corn, six goats, a cow, eight sheep and a number of pigs. His was the largest holding of sheep in the colony, a fact probably explained by his trade as a weaver. His widow, Mary, was awarded custody of her two children with Browne; those of Browne and Martha Ford were apprenticed out. However, when they turned seventeen, they asked the Plymouth court to assign their custody to their uncle, John Browne, a weaver who was living near the Aldens in Duxbury. He was Peter Browne's younger brother, born in Dorking in 1600, who had followed him to the colony in about 1632[2]. He settled and married Phoebe Harding in Plymouth in early 1634.

The economy of the settlement was agricultural, based on food crops, the produce of kitchen gardens and the husbanding of the pigs and goats that had come over on the *Mayflower* and the cattle and sheep that followed on subsequent ships. Farming was supplemented

---

[1] A number of Dorking residents travelled to the New World at much the same time as John Browne: Christopher Hussey sailed for New England in 1633; William Dudley and his wife Jane of Ockley settled in Connecticut in 1639 and Stockdale Coddington, who owned the house known as Godfreys on West Street, crossed with his wife Hannah to New England in the 1640s.

by hunting for game and fishing. The women of the settlement were responsible for milking and the production of cheese and butter. Far from any shop or trading centre, the colonists had to be self-sufficient, making their own clothes, barrels and agricultural tools. John Alden worked as a cooper and was involved in the fur trade; Priscilla would have been responsible for the kitchen garden, for sewing, weaving cloth, cooking, caring for her large family and probably also for brewing the household beverages.

To ensure law and order, the colonists organised themselves into a form of government, with Edward Bradford the official head of the colony. By the time of the move to Duxbury, John Alden was in his thirties and he increasingly took on roles of responsibility within the community. From 1632 to 1640 and from 1650 to 1686 he was an assistant to the governor, one of a number of men who formed a senior advisory council and who were also the senior magistrates in the colony. He also served as deputy governor twice and was the colony's treasurer in 1656, 1657 and 1658. For a period in the 1640s he was Duxbury's elected representative to the colony's General Court, (which was more a legislative body than a general court). He was also responsible, alongside Standish, for negotiating with the Wampanoag to establish land rights for the settlers. His wife's wealth and social position very likely helped him achieve his status in the colony.

Alden was also involved in setting up a fur trading post on the Kennebec river. In 1634, he was jailed in Boston when rivalry with the neighbouring colony spilled over into a fight. This dispute over lucrative fur trading saw one of the Plymouth colonists killed and a revenge killing of his attacker. Alden was not involved in the fight but was arrested as a senior member of the New Plymouth colony. His old rival, Captain Standish, was sent to negotiate his release.

Priscilla's older brother, William, joined her in the colony in 1636, fifteen years after the death of their father, (step) mother and younger brother. The teenager that he had last seen in Dorking was now the mother of seven children. William had inherited his father's land in Massachusetts and he travelled to the colony with his own daughter, Sarah, and set up home there. (His older children stayed in England, just as he had done when his father sailed.) He returned to England at least once; in 1649 he was one of sixteen citizens of London (including Edward Winslow) who founded a Society for the Propagation of the Gospel in New England. Its aim was to spread the word of God among the native peoples by preaching in their own languages and founding schools for their children. Sarah Mullins married three times in the colony but had no children. William junior probably married again in New England and died there in 1672. His sister, Sarah Blunden, was the only one of William Mullins' children never to travel to the colony.

John and Priscilla's children went on to establish their own families; between them they produced over seventy children, populating the colony. With time-consuming commitments to the government of the colony and with ten children to support, Alden never became wealthy, though the court repaid his commitment with grants of land which he was able to distribute amongst his sons before his death. Living to a great age, John Alden was the last survivor of the Mayflower Compact. He died in Duxbury on 12th September 1687, having survived 67 years in the colony. Priscilla is thought to have pre-deceased him. Both are buried in the Myles Standish Burial Ground at Duxbury.

Some of John and Priscilla's descendants continued to live on John and Priscilla's original Duxbury land, building (or enlarging) a house in about 1700 that still stands today as the Alden House Historic

The graves of John and Priscilla Alden in the Myles Standish Burial Ground in Duxbury, Massachusetts. (Image Creative Commons Licence Swampyank)

Site. Together with the nearby archaeological remains of the earlier house where they raised their family, it constitutes the John and Priscilla Alden Family Sites National Historic Landmark. Descendants lived in the Alden House until the early 1920s. The house was purchased by the Alden Kindred of America, Inc. in 1907. The land on which the house sits has been continuously owned by the Alden family for nearly four hundred years.

Of all the *Mayflower* families, the Mulllins/Aldens are thought to have the greatest number of descendants living today. When, 150 years after the arrival of the *Mayflower*, the peoples of the original thirteen American colonies declared independence from Britain, one of John and Priscilla's descendants was amongst those who framed that declaration. Founding Father John Adams (1735-1826) was the great-great-grandson of the girl from Dorking. He was the first United States ambassador to the United Kingdom and became the second president of the United States in 1797. His son, John Quincy Adams (1767-1848), also served as United States ambassador to the United Kingdom and was the nation's sixth president. His grandson Charles Francis Adams also served as ambassador to the United Kingdom.

The Alden House in Duxbury, Massachusetts, pictured in 2010. (Reproduced by permission of the Alden Kindred of America)

The weaver, the shoemaker and the mother of a nation

When he sailed in 1620, William Mullins could have had no idea of the significance that would later be attached to those who voyaged on the *Mayflower.* Other than his property in Dorking, nothing personal remains to tell us about his life; there is no diary, memoir or cache of letters by which we might know him. The blue plaque on the front of the building makes no mention of the others from the town who accompanied him. The sole survivor of the Mullins party, the teenager who survived the crossing and the colony's first winter and went on to face the challenge of bringing up ten children 3,000 miles from home, does not merit even a mention. However, in the United States, it is the girl from West Street who is revered, the site of her home a national monument: Priscilla, the Pilgrim Mother.

Such is the renown of Priscilla Mullins in the United States that figurines have been produced in her image. (From the collection of Dorking Museum. Image by Royston Williamson)

The children of Priscilla Mullins & John Alden

Elizabeth (born c1624 or 1625 and died 1717) was the mother of thirteen children; she lived to 94.

John (born before May 1627 and died 1702) was the father of fourteen children. A sea captain involved with the neighbouring Massachusetts Bay Colony, he was accused of witchcraft on a visit to Salem where he spent time in jail.

Joseph (born after May 1627 and died 1697) was a farmer and the father of seven children.

Priscilla (birth and death dates unknown); unmarried.

Jonathan (born c1633 and died 1697) fathered six children.

Sarah (born between 1630 and 1640 and had died by 1688) married the son of Miles Standish and was the mother of eight children.

Ruth (born c1637 and died 1674) had seven children, one of them the grandmother of future President John Adams.

Mary (birth and death dates unknown); unmarried.

Rebecca (born before 1640 and died after 1696) was the mother of nine children.

David (born between 1645 and 1650 and had died by 1719) was the father of six children.

The Aldens' great-great-grandson, John Adams (1735-1828). Lawyer, diplomat and Independence leader, he was the United States' first vice-president and second president. Thomas Jefferson (1743-1826) was his vice-president. Painting by Gilbert Stuart. (From the collection of the National Gallery of Art)

The weaver, the shoemaker and the mother of a nation

John Alden Jr and the Salem witch trials

The *Mayflower* settlement was the first successful permanent English settlement in the Americas. In the coming years thousands crossed the ocean, a mass emigration from a country with a population of only three and a half million. It is estimated that by 1640 there were 15,000 more settlers in New England alone, brought on scores of ships. The area around Plymouth is dotted with familiar English names: Boston, Cambridge, Barnstable, Sandwich, Harwich, Chatham, Taunton, Rochester, Falmouth… truly a New England.

Increasing settlement put pressure on natural resources and open war eventually broke out between individual colonists and native inhabitants, and between individual colonies, a situation that was complicated by rival French interests in what became known as New England and New France. John and Priscilla Alden's eldest son played a part in these territorial wars and it was this that brought him to Salem in the 1690s.

John Jr, grew up with his parents in Duxbury and became a sea captain and a merchant in the thriving town of Boston. In the 1680s, he took a military command in what became known as King William's War, fought between the English and French and their various native allies for control of the territories that form northern New England and the southern Canadian seaboard. In 1692, when he was in his sixties, he went to Quebec to ransom some British prisoners held there by native American tribes allied to the French. On the way back he stopped at the town of Salem in Massachusetts, where he was accused of witchcraft. One of his accusers was Mercy Lewis who had been orphaned during a native American raid on her village in Maine; it has been suggested that she accused Alden in a desire for revenge against community leaders who had failed to protect her community. Alden does not seem to have had any personal contact with his accusers and much of the 'evidence' against him seems to have been tittle tattle about trading with the native population.

Alden was convicted during the Salem Witch Trials in May 1692 and incarcerated in Boston. In mid-September he escaped and fled back to Duxbury, where a large family of brothers, nephews and nieces were still living. He is alleged to have woken his family in the dead of night, saying that he was *'flying from the Devil, and the Devil was after him'*. His escape was a wise move, since one of his co-accused was executed shortly after his departure. He hid out with family until, as he put it, *'the public had reclaimed the use of its reason'*. He was later cleared by proclamation and published an account of the trials, recording the way that the girls, who he referred to as *'juggling wenches',* had behaved and the response of the judges who seemed convinced by their fits. He died in Boston ten years later.

The weaver, the shoemaker and the mother of a nation

The Mullins family is still celebrated in Dorking and on occasion actors depict William and Priscilla on guided walks through the town where they lived. (Images reproduced by permission of Royston Williamson)

The weaver, the shoemaker and the mother of a nation

Detail from *Procession of the Ancestors of the Alden Family* (1905) by Philip Dadd. The paintings is structured as a procession depicting the family line of one particular *Mayflower* family and was commissioned by a descendent of Priscilla Mullins and John Alden. The procession depicts John Carver and Governor William Bradford, followed by William Brewster and Myles Standish, and, behind them, Priscilla Mullins and John Alden (under the oak tree). In the background a joint wedding ceremony in the colony is depicted. (Reproduced by permission of Richard Miller)

Appendix 1

Mayflower Passenger List

The list of passengers was written 30 years after the voyage, in 1651, by William Bradford, the colony's second governor, best known for his memoir of the Leiden congregation and the Plymouth Colony. He was writing from memory so in some cases forenames or surnames are not recorded.

John Alden
Isaac and Mary Allerton and children Bartholomew, Remember and Mary
John Allerton
John and Eleanor Billington and children John and Francis
William and Dorothy Bradford
William and Mary Brewster and children Love and Wrestling
Richard Bitteridge
Peter Browne
William Butten
Robert Carter
John and Katherine Carver
James and Mrs Chilton and their daughter Mary
Richard Clarke
Francis Cooke and son John
Humility Cooper
John Crackstone and son John
Edward Doty
Francis and Sarah Eaton and son Samuel
Thomas English
Moses Fletcher
Edward and Mrs Fuller and son Samuel
Richard Gardiner
John Goodman
William Holbeck
John Hook
Stephen and Elizabeth Hopkins and children Constance, Giles and Damaris (son Oceanus born on board)
John Howland
John Langmore
William Latham

Edward Leister
Edmund Margesson
Christopher and Mary Martin
Desire Minter
Ellen, Jasper, Richard and Mary More (unaccompanied children)
William and Alice Mullins and children Priscilla and Joseph
Degory Priest
Solomon Prower
John and Alice Rinsdale
Thomas Rogers and son Joseph
Henry Samson
George Soule
Miles and Rose Standish
Elias Story
Edward Thompson
Edward and Agnes Tilley
John and Joan Tilley and daughter Elizabeth
Thomas and Mrs Tinker and son
William Trevore
John Turner and two sons
Richard Warren
William and Susannah White and son Resolved (son Peregrine was born on board)
Roger Wilder
Thomas Williams
Edward and Elizabeth Winslow
Mr Ely
Dorothy (John Carver's maidservant)

Appendix 2

Transcription of the Will of William Mullins

In the name of God Amen: I comit my soule to God that gave it and my bodie to earth from whence I came. Also I give my goodes as followeth That forty poundes wch is in the hand of goodman Woodes I give my Wife tenn pounds, my sonne Joseph tenn pounds, my daughter Priscilla tenn poundes, and my eldest sonne tenn poundes Also I give to my eldest sonne all my debtes, bondes, bills (onelye that forty poundes excepted in the handes of goodman Wood) given as aforesaid, Withall the stock in his owne handes To my eldest daughter I give tenn shillings to be paied out of my sonnes stock Furthermore that goodes I have in Virginia as followeth To my wife Alice halfe my goodes & to Joseph and Priscilla the other halfe equallie to be devided betweene them. Also I give xxj dozen shoes, and thirteene paire of bootes wch I give into the Companies hands for Forty poundes at seaven years and if they like them at that rate If it be thought to deare as my Overseers shall thinck good And if they like them at that rate at the Devident I shall have Nyne shares Whereof I give as followeth twoe to my wife, twoe to my sonne William, twoe to my sonne Joseph, twoe to my daughter Priscilla, and one to the Companie Allsoe if my sonne William Will come to Virginia I give him my share of land furdermore I give to my twoe Overseers Mr John Carver and Mr Williamson, twentye shillings appece to see this my Will performed Desiringe them that they Would have an eye over my Wife and children to be as fathers and freinds to them, Allsoe to have a speciall eye to my Man Robert wch hathe not so approved himselfe as I would he should have done.

This is a Copye of Mr Mullens his Will of all particulars he hath given In witness whereof I have sett my hande

Thomas Ridley*, John Carver, Giles Heale, Christofer Joanes

> Mullins' is the only surviving will from one of the passengers who died during the colonists' first winter. His name is spelled 'Mullens' but spelling was not standardised in this period. The will was carried back to England when the *Mayflower* returned. Mullins did not appoint an executor in his will and there remains some question as to whom probate was awarded. Two copies of the will were made. One, registered at the Prerogative Court of Canterbury, records that probate was issued on 23rd July 1621 to Mullins' married daughter, Sarah Blunden. The other, registered with the Archdeaconry Court of Surrey, states that it was issued on 1st June 1621 to his son, William Mullins Jr.
>
> *The name of Thomas Ridley only appears in the copy registered with the ACS.
>
> Mullins was described as *'late of Dorking in the county of Surrey, but deceased in parts beyond the seas'*.

Appendix 3

Abridged version of THE PROBABLE ENGLISH ORIGIN OF *MAYFLOWER* PASSENGER PETER BROWNE, AND HIS ASSOCIATION WITH *MAYFLOWER* PASSENGER WILLIAM MULLINS by Caleb Johnson, published in *The American Genealogist* Vol. 79, No. 3, July 2004, pp 161-178.

Although there have occasionally been claims made about the ancestry of *Mayflower* passenger Peter Browne[3], nothing of any significance has been published to document his English origins. Robert Anderson's *Great Migration Begins* simply gives his origins as unknown,[4] and *Mayflower Families for Five Generations* states that "[n]othing is known of Peter Brown's background."[5]

However, several pieces of information are known about Peter Browne from American records that make it possible to examine English records with a more critical eye.

Peter Browne's age can be roughly estimated from several facts. First, he was a signer of the so-called "*Mayflower* Compact" on 11 November 1620, so almost certainly had reached 21 years of age by that time.[6] He married the widow Martha (--) Ford, who had come to Plymouth in 1621 as one of the only women on board the ship *Fortune*. Their marriage would have occurred sometime between the 1623 Division of Land (where "widow Foord" received 4 acres),[7] and the 1627 Division of Cattle (where Peter is

---

[3] Leon Clark Hills published a purported royal ancestry for Peter Browne in *History and Genealogy of the Mayflower Planters and First Comers to ye Olde Colonie*, Cape Cod Ser., 2 vols. (Washington, D.C., 1936-41), 2:131-32, which Robert S. Wakefield called "clearly invalid" in *The Mayflower Descendant* [MD] 43(1993):13. Likewise, Charles E. Banks in his *English Ancestry and Homes of the Pilgrim Fathers* (Boston, 1929), 41, mentions that there was a man named Peter Brown taxed in 1624 in Great Burstead, Essex, which has led some to assume that this parish must be the origin of the *Mayflower* passenger.

[4] Robert Charles Anderson, *The Great Migration Begins*, 3 vols. (Boston, 1995), 1:259 (hereafter cited as Anderson, *Great Migration Begins*).

[5] Robert S. Wakefield, *Mayflower Families for Five Generations, Vol. 7: Peter Brown*, 2nd ed. (Plymouth, Mass., 2002), 2 (hereafter cited as *MF 5Gs: Browne*).

[6] Nathaniel Morton was the first to list the names of the signers in his *New England's Memorial* (London, 1669).

[7] Nathaniel B. Shurtleff and David Pulsifer, eds., *Records of the Colony of New Plymouth in New England*, 12 vols. in 10 (Boston, 1855-61), 12:4 (hereafter cited as Shurtleff and Pulsifer, *Plym. Col. Recs.*).

listed with wife Martha and their eldest daughter, Mary Browne, along with stepchildren John and Martha Ford).[8] From these facts, we can see that Peter Browne was born before 1599, but since he was married and had his first daughter by early 1627, he probably would not have been born too many years prior to that.

Following the birth of daughter Mary in late 1626 or early 1627, Peter and Martha Brown had another daughter, Priscilla, born about 1628.[9] Martha Browne died sometime shortly thereafter, and Peter remarried to a woman named Mary, whose identity has not been discovered. With wife Mary, he had a daughter Rebecca, born about 1631, and another child, who was born about 1633 and who apparently died young because he or she did not participate in the division of Peter Browne's lands.

Peter Browne himself died in the autumn of 1633, following what may have been a lengthy illness. Earlier that year, Peter had been fined 3s. on 1 January and 2 January for failing to show up at Plymouth's court session, and on 7 January he was sued by Dr. Samuel Fuller for "divers accounts...wherein they differ." The court sent them to arbitration by Robert Hicks and Francis Cooke.[10] Following Peter's death later that year, an inventory of his estate was taken, dated 10 October 1633. He owed the widow of Dr. Samuel Fuller an unstated amount for "1 peck malt & purgac," and Peter Browne's widow, Mary, also owed an unstated amount to "the Surgion for letting her man bloud."[11] Purgatives and bloodletting were the doctor and surgeon's torturous attempts to rebalance the four humours.

Widow Mary was allowed by the court to maintain her own two biological children by Peter, but her stepchildren, Mary and Priscilla Browne, were given a £15 trust and fostered out to John Doane and William Gilson, respectively, until the girls reached the age of 17.[12] When Mary and Priscilla Browne turned 17, they both requested that the Plymouth Colony Court

---

[8] Shurtleff and Pulsifer, *Plym. Col. Recs.*, 12:11.
[9] The birth years for daughters Mary and Priscilla are based on their ages from Shurtleff and Pulsifer, *Plym. Col. Recs.*, 2:76, 86 (when they had turned 17 years old), and by Mary's appearance in the 22 May 1627 Division of Cattle at Plymouth (Shurtleff and Pulsifer, *Plym. Col. Recs.*, 12:11).
[10] Shurtleff and Pulsifer, *Plym. Col. Recs.*, 1:5, 7, 8.
[11] C. H. Simmons, ed., *Plymouth Colony Records, Volume 1: Wills and Inventories, 1633-1669* (Camden, Maine, 1996), 21-23.
[12] Shurtleff and Pulsifer, *Plym. Col. Recs.*, 1:18-19.

assign their custody over to their uncle, John Browne of Duxbury, until they "shalbe marryed, or thought fitt to marry."[13]

John Browne of Duxbury, thus, was Peter Browne's brother, which is another important piece of the puzzle. John Browne arrived about 1632, and married Phoebe Harding at Plymouth on 26 March 1634.[14] *The Great Migration Begins* gives this John Browne one child, Remember, who married Josiah Wormall.[15] *Mayflower Families for Five Generations: Peter Brown* mentions a daughter Mary,[16] but this is a confusion with a contemporaneous man named John Browne then living in Plymouth. Confusion about his children aside, what is important is that John Browne of Duxbury was Peter Browne's brother, and that he was presumably a younger brother, based on marriage dates.

In addition, John Browne of Duxbury's occupation should be noted. A land transaction found in the Plymouth Colony Records, dated 8 June 1650, mentions "John Browne of Duxburrow in the Colonie aforesaid weaver," and goes on to mention "land which appertained unto the Children of Peeter Browne brother unto John Browne aforesaid."[17] So Peter Browne's brother John was a weaver by trade.

For those who are familiar with *Mayflower* genealogy, the parish of Dorking, co. Surrey, England, will be immediately recognized: it is well known as the home parish of William and Alice Mullins, who came on the *Mayflower* with children Priscilla and Joseph Mullins. Several years ago, while checking the parish register of Dorking, co. Surrey, in my behalf, for *Mullins* entries, Leslie Mahler noticed the baptisms of two brothers named Peter and John Browne. The Peter Browne whom I propose as the *Mayflower* passenger was baptized there on 26 January 1594/5, the son of William Browne. It seems Peter Browne's baptism was sitting right under the noses of *Mayflower* researchers all along.

---

[13] Shurtleff and Pulsifer, *Plym. Col. Recs.*, 2:76 [Mary], 2:89 [Priscilla]. The quoted phrase is from the record of Mary Browne's acquiring a new guardian; the record for Priscilla explicitly calls John Browne her uncle.
[14] Shurtleff and Pulsifer, *Plym. Col. Recs.*, 1:26.
[15] Anderson, *Great Migration Begins*, 1:257-59. For information on Josiah Wormall, see Donna Valley Russell and Alicia Crane Williams, "Descendants of Joseph Wormall of Scituate," MD 43(1993): 152-55. The will of John Browne of Duxbury is found in Shurtleff and Pulsifer, *Plym. Col. Recs.*, 4, pt. 2:128.
[16] *MF 5Gs: Browne*, 3.
[17] Shurtleff and Pulsifer, *Plym. Col. Recs.*, 12:186.

William Browne the father was probably the William Browne who was baptized in Dorking on 25 April 1559. He married around 1587 – based on the baptismal date of his first known child – but the name of his wife or wives has not been discovered. A William Browne was named in 1583/4 and 1596 muster lists for Dorking, in 1583/4 being referred to as an archer "of the second sort," and in 1596 being referred to as a billman.[18]

William Browne was buried in Dorking on 2 June 1605; added to the burial record in a later – but still seventeenth-century – hand is an additional word, perhaps an indication of his occupation: "clarke." No will is found for him in the Archdeaconry of Surrey or in the Prerogative Court of Canterbury. Unfortunately, many of the wills for the year 1605 in the Archdeaconry of Surrey are lost. William is named, however, in the will of his brother Thomas Browne of Dorking, yeoman, dated 20 February 1596/7 and proved on 10 September 1597.[19] In the will, Thomas mentions "Alice my wife," son Michael, daughter Elizabeth, and "the child that my wife nowe goeth w[i]thall."[20] Thomas Browne stated that "yf I have but one sonne my will is that my brother Will[ia]m Browne shall have the howse that he nowe dwelleth in." Perhaps unfortunately for William, the unborn child was a boy.

On 20 September 19 James I [1621], Michael and John Browne sold to William Wood their two tenements consisting of a "curtelage and garden scituat in le ~~Weststreet~~ Southstreet now devided into tenem[en]ts between the tenem[en]t or capitall mess[u]age of Sr Ri: Sondes knight on the west The land sometimes Wm Elliot north, a mess[uage] late Tho: Willottes est, and the K[ings] highewaye or Southstreet afores[ai]d south."[21] Their property had been purchased by their father Thomas Browne "musicon of Dorking" on 20 March 25 Elizabeth [1583/4] from Richard Holland.[22]

The children of William Browne can be identified from the parish registers of Dorking, except for eldest daughter Jane, who was baptized in

---

[18] *Surrey Musters (Taken from the Loseley Mss.)*, Surrey Record Soc., 3(London 1914-19), hereafter cited as *Surrey Musters*.

[19] Will of Thomas Browne, Archdeaconry of Surrey, London Metropolitan Archives, DW/PA/7/7 f.144; DW/PA/5/1597/16.

[20] Dorking parish registers show the bps. of Thomas Browne's children Joane (bp. 28 March 1588), Elizabeth (bp. 25 April 1591), Michael (bp. 18 Nov. 1593), and John (bp. 17 April 1597). Thomas Browne himself was bur. on 16 Aug. 1597.

[21] Survey of the Manor of Dorking, Arundel Castle Archives, MD2341. The record is archived under the date 26 May 1608, but contains entries dating through 1622.

[22] Survey of the Manor of Dorking, Arundel Castle Archives, MD2341.

the parish of Betchworth, the neighboring parish to the east. All dates are from Dorking parish registers unless otherwise noted:

    i JANE BROWNE, bp. Betchworth, Surrey, 15 Sept. 1588,[23] bur. Dorking, 18 Jan. 1636/7; m. there, 29 June 1610, JOHN HAMMON.
        Children: 1. *Anne Hammon*, bp. 19 Sept. 1611. 2. *Susan Hammon*, bp. 12 Aug. 1613, probably d. young. 3. *Jane Hammon*, bp. 27 Aug. 1615, probably d. young. 4. *Susan Hammon* (again), bp. 8 Sept. 1616. 5. *Jane Hammon* (again), bp. 14 Feb. 1618[/9].

    ii THOMAS BROWNE, bp. 22 Oct. 1590. His marriage record is not found in Dorking or Betchworth. He is, however, almost certainly the Thomas Browne of Dorking who had children bp. and/or bur. there: 1. *John Browne*, bur. 13 June 1616. 2. *Alice Browne*, bp. 13 April 1617, bur. 15 April 1617. 3. *Thomas Browne*, bp. 29 July 1618, bur. 10 Aug. 1618. 4. *Thomas Browne* (again), bp. 17 June 1619, bur. 20 June 1619. 5. *Thomas Browne* (again), bur. 4 Dec. 1621. 6. *Thomas Browne* (again), bp. 5 Nov. 1622. 7. *Mary Browne*, bp. ("Marie") Dec. 1625, bur. 26 July 1642. 8. *Hannah Browne*, bp. 28 Oct. 1628, bur. 3 April 1631. 9 *Susan Browne*, bp. 24 April 1631.

    iii PETER BROWNE, bp. 26 Jan. 1594/5. He is the proposed *Mayflower* passenger. No marriage or burial record for Peter is found in Dorking.

    iv SAMUEL BROWNE, bp. 18 April 1598, bur. 1 Feb. 1624/5; m. (1) 18 April 1620, DOROTHY KEMPE, m. (2) 2 July 1624, ADREH RUTTLAN. His widow Adreh m. (2) 17 July 1625, John Willatt. Samuel apparently had no children by either marriage.

    v JOHN BROWNE, bp. 29 June 1600. He is the proposed weaver of Duxbury, Mass. There is no marriage or burial record that appears to pertain to this John Browne of Dorking. A Nicholas, son of John Browne, was bp. in 1633, but there was another John Browne in the parish.

    vi JAMES BROWNE, bp. 24 July 1603, bur. 3 Jan. 1644/5; m. Oct. 1628 ELIZABETH HUETT.
        Children: 1. *James Browne*, bp. 10 April 1631, bur. 28 July 1635. 2. *Peter Browne*, bp. 16 March 1633/4. 3. *James Browne* (again), bp. 23 Oct. 1636, bur. 26 March 1638. 4. *Ambrose*

---

[23] Extract from the parish registers of Betchworth, Surrey History Centre.

Browne, bp. 10 Feb. 1638/9, bur. 30 Dec. 1640. 5. *Samuel Browne*, bp. 16 June 1642.

As can be seen, Peter Browne of Dorking had a younger brother John, just as *Mayflower* passenger Peter Browne did. Both Peter and John Browne disappear from Dorking records, whereas their siblings Jane, Thomas, Samuel, and James do not.

Two other important pieces of evidence in support of this theory are the burial records of Peter and John's siblings, Samuel and James Browne. The Dorking burial record of Samuel Browne, dated 1 February 1624/5, reads "Samuel Browne weaver buried." The burial record of James Browne of Dorking, dated 3 January 1644/5, reads "James Browne a weaver was buried." Samuel and James Browne were therefore both weavers – the same occupation held by John Browne of Duxbury.

Finally, it cannot be overlooked that Peter Browne of the *Mayflower* gave one of his daughters the fairly uncommon name *Priscilla*; and *Mayflower* passenger William Mullins of Dorking also had a daughter named Priscilla. If indeed both families were from Dorking and both named daughters Priscilla, it would seem highly probably that the two families shared some social or familial connection. An examination of the Mullins family of Dorking is therefore in order.

MAYFLOWER PASSENGER WILLIAM MULLINS OF DORKING, SURREY
The English origin of William Mullins has been known for more than one hundred years, as his Dorking origin is clearly apparent in his nuncupative will dated 2 April 1621, first published in *The Mayflower Descendant* in 1899. The original will, signed by Plymouth's first governor John Carver, the *Mayflower*'s master Christopher Jones, and the *Mayflower*'s ship surgeon Giles Heale, still survives. A contemporary copy recorded at the Prerogative Court of Canterbury also exists.[24] The will and its associated probate administration mention wife Alice, eldest son William, eldest daughter Sarah Blunden, and the two children he brought with him on the *Mayflower*,

---

[24] A transcription can be found in MD 1(1899):231-32 and again at 44(1994):19. A transcription can also be found on my website, *mayflowerhistory.com*. A facsimile reprint of the original is in my now out-of-print compendium *The Complete Works of the Mayflower Pilgrims* (Vancouver, Wash., 2002). A scan of the PCC copy of the will can be ordered online at *documentsonline.pro.gov.uk*.

Priscilla and Joseph. Also mentioned is a servant Robert Carter,[25] and one "goodman Wood" who was holding a fairly substantial sum of money (£40) belonging to Mullins. Overseers named were John Carver and "Mr. Williamson." John Carver was the governor of Plymouth, but "Mr. Williamson" remains unidentified.[26]

Although William Mullins's origins have been so widely known for more than a hundred years, nobody has really bothered to perform a more thorough investigation of the records he left behind in Dorking. To date, the main contributions to Mullins scholarship are two pamphlets published locally in Dorking, England, [27] and a summary and analysis of the current state of knowledge by Alicia Crane Williams.[28] While valuable contributions, the pamphlets are generally undocumented and overlook some important sources of local information.

The parentage and ancestry of William Mullins have not been conclusively proven. The Mullins family may have been living in Dorking for a considerable period of time prior to William Mullins himself, as the Dorking manor court rolls between 1454 and 1458 mention a Peter and Isabel Moleyn on several occasions.[29]

The Dorking parish registers are unfortunately defective for the years 1572 through 1578 – the time period in which we would expect William to

---

[25] There was a Carter family in Dorking that could be the origin of this *Mayflower* passenger as well, although nothing obvious stood out during the course of this research. Of some interest is the marriage of Thomas Carter to Jane Bothell in Dorking on 3 April 1648. Jane Bothell was the daughter of Ephraim and Susan Bothell. As will be seen later in this article, the Mullins family had close associations with the Bothell family.

[26] John G. Hunt, "Master Williamson of the Mayflower" *National Genealogical Society Quarterly* 62(1974): 88-90, suggests that "Mr. Williamson" may have been a pseudonym for Elder William Brewster, then a fugitive from English authorities for having printed and distributed unauthorized religious pamphlets and books in England. Charles Banks, in his *English Ancestry and Homes of the Pilgrim Fathers*, speculated that master Williamson may have been one of the *Mayflower*'s seamen, whom he called "Andrew Williamson." In Dorking there was a Percival Williamson who married Mary Pilson in 1581. However, there are no apparent connections to the Mullins family, although his daughter Winifred Williamson married John Rutland in 1605, presumably a relative of Samuel Browne's 2nd wife, Adreh Rutland.

[27] John Walker, *William Mullins* (Dorking, 1973); Pam Hunter, *William Mullins: Pilgrim Father* (Dorking, 2000).

[28] Alicia Crane Williams, "The Mullins Family," MD44(1994): 39-44.

[29] Transcripts of Dorking Manor Court Rolls, Vol. C [1454-58], Surrey History Centre, pp.125, 130, 144-45.

have been baptized. However, there was only one Mullins family in Dorking that was having children during this time period: the John Mullins who married Joan Bridger there on 8 July 1571. Most of their children would have fallen into the "black hole" in the registers. On 23 September 1582, we see the baptism of their last child, Edward Mullins. On 4 February 1583/4, a Mullins (no Christian name given) was buried. We can reasonably assume this burial record was for John Mullins the father, because the next Mullins burial record in the registers, on 8 July 1584, was recorded as the "son of widow Mullins." And since son Edward Mullins appears in no subsequent Dorking records, we can speculate that this was the unnamed son who was buried. The following year, on 1 November 1585, the widow Joane Mullins was remarried to Vyncent Benham.[30]

Two Mullinses appear in later Dorking records; they are assumed to be unrecorded children of John and Joan (Bridger) Mullins. They are the *Mayflower* passenger, William Mullins, and John Mullins.

John Mullins only appears in two Dorking records that I have yet discovered. On 6 October 4 James I [1606], he was listed as one of the residents of Eastborough, Dorking, his elected tithingman being William Wood.[31] And on 17 October 1614, he buried a daughter named Sarah. Another John Mullins, perhaps son of John, brother of William, appears in Dorking records from 1636-43, with the burial of wife Ursula in 1636, a remarriage to Sarah Rinning in 1637, a remarriage to Joan Gammon in 1639, and a burial in 1643 in which he is called a shoemaker.[32]

Future *Mayflower* passenger William Mullins appears in a number of Dorking records, so more is learned about him. The first mention of William Mullins occurs on 4 October 1595, when he was fined 2*d*., presumably for not

---

[30] Alicia Crane Williams made this Joane Mullins a sister of John Mullins in her article mentioned above. However, given the timing – coming a year after the apparent death of John Mullins – this almost certainly is the widow remarrying and not an otherwise unrecorded sister of John. No will for Vincent Benham was located in the Archdeaconry of Surrey.

[31] Arundel Castle Archives, Dorking Court Rolls M809 / 6 Oct. 4 Jas. I.

[32] The two Dorking pamphlets attempt to make this John Mullins the same man as the brother of William Mullins. However, given that his third wife Joan remarried in 1644 and had several children by her new husband John Foster, she would seem to be an unlikely third wife of a man of 60 or older. I suspect all these records are for a younger John Mullins.

attending the manorial court session of that date. His place of residence was given as Chippingborough, Dorking.[33]

William Mullins disappears from Dorking records between October 1595 and September 1604, exactly the time period in which he would have been marrying and having his children. William Mullins's marriage and the baptisms of his children are not found in Dorking parish registers. The Dorking muster list of 1596 is a fairly complete enumeration of adult men living in Dorking, yet the list contains no entry for Mullins.[34] His fine for non-appearance at the 1595 court session, his absence from the 1596 muster list, his absence from the parish registers when he would have been marrying and having children, his relocation to a different neighbourhood when he reappears in Dorking, all seem to hint that he removed from Dorking for a period of time. Conveniently enough, a William Mullins shows up on a muster list at Stoke-near-Guildford, Surrey, in 1596.[35] I have not been able to find any Mullins families residing in the vicinity of Stoke or Guildford during this time period that could have produced another man of the same name. Then, on 11 December 1598, an Elizabeth, daughter of William Mullins, was baptized at Holy Trinity, Guildford. Most unfortunately, the parish registers for Stoke do not exist prior to 1662, and there are no further Mullins entries in any of the parishes of Guildford that could help confirm the identity of this William Mullins. Following the baptism of Elizabeth, no further records for this William Mullins are seen in Guildford or Stoke.

William Mullins reappears in Eastborough, a different neighbourhood in Dorking, on 5 October 2 James I [1604], when the Dorking manor court rolls record: *Et in officiu decenarij de Estburgh eliger' Willm Mullens qui etiam iurat' est* ["And in the office of tithingman of Eastborough they have chosen William Mullins, who is also sworn"].[36] As the elected tithingman, William Mullins was responsible for representing a frankpledge, a group of about ten households, usually families and neighbours. The group was collectively bonded to the king for their good behaviour. On 19 September 3 James I [1605], William Mullins, tithingman in Eastborough, was summoned to appear before a jury, where his frankpledge was apparently fined 3s. 7d. "per capita." It is unclear what the fine was for, but it appears that the members

---

[33] Arundel Castle Archives, Dorking Court Rolls M809 / 4 Oct. 37 Eliz.
[34] *Surrey Musters*, Surrey Record Soc., 3:23.
[35] *Surrey Musters*, Surrey Record Soc., 3:238.
[36] Arundel Castle Archives, Dorking Court Rolls M809 / 5 Oct. 2 Jas. I.

of the frankpledge were Robert Sparkes, William Dendye,[37] Robert Banyster, John Man, William Tudham,[38] Innocent Sheffield,[39] Ralph Arnold, Richard Steare, Simon Cookes, Simon White, John Browne,[40] and William Wood.

In 1612 William Mullins appears in a trio of records. On 30 March 1612, he witnessed the will of John Wood, signing the document with a mark and not a signature.[41] On 20 December 1612, William Mullins, shoemaker, was named as an overseer to the estate of widow Jane Hammon.[42] Her will was proved on 27 September 1615. And on 28 December 1612, William Mullins purchased from John Jettor, "by Indenture of bargaine and sale and pole deed" for £122 "w[i]th a bond of 200£ thereupon," a tenement "in the West Streete in Dorkinge nowe converted into [*blank*] ten[emen]tes w[i]th a barne and backside late John Sheffeildes and after John Jetter."[43] The land was described in words such as "now being occupied."

William Mullins remained there for seven years, and then in May 1619, apparently in preparation for his voyage on the *Mayflower* the following year, he sold his manor holding to Ephraim Bothell for £180.[44] He

---

[37] William Dendy, son of John Dendy, m. Ann Sparke on 26 Nov. 1599 in Dorking; presumably she is a relative of the preceding Robert Sparkes.

[38] The will of Richard Tudham of Dorking, butcher, dated 11 Jan. 1605/6, proved 14 Feb. 1605/6, mentions "kinsman William, son of Simon Tudham." Also mentioned is Richard, son of William Symon; godson Richard son of Ralph Arnold; and godson John son of Stockdale Coddington, among others. The will was witnessed by Stockdale Coddington (Archdeaconry of Surrey, DW/PA/5/1605/91.)

[39] Innocent Sheffield's will, dated July 1617 and proved 27 Aug. 1619, mentions wife Mary, and was witnessed by John Wood (Archdeaconry of Surrey, DW/PA/5/1619/99.)

[40] The will of Emma Clarke of Dorking, widow, dated 19 Aug. 1607, proved 17 Feb. 1607/8, mentions Sarah daughter of Henry Browne; the wife of John Browne; executor William Symon, butcher, and witness John Wood the elder (Archdeaconry of Surrey, DW/PA/5/1607/27). The will of Christian Browne of Dorking, singlewoman, dated 29 Nov. 1603 and proved 2 Jan. 1603/4, mentions brother John Browne, sister Joan Browne, and her master Richard Tudham, with overseer William Symon (Archdeaconry of Surrey, DW/PA/5/1603/22).

[41] Will of John Wood (Archdeaconry of Surrey, DW/PA/7/8 ff229r-230v; DW/PA/1612/175). The original at the London Metropolitan Archives was viewed to determine whether Mullins signed by a mark.

[42] Will of Jane Hammon (Archdeaconry of Surrey, DW/PA/7/9 ff 135v-136r; DW/PA/5/1615/56).

[43] Arundel Castle Archives, Survey of the manor of Dorking, MD2341 / 26 May 1608. The document is archived under the date 26 May 1608, but contains entries through 1622.

[44] Arundel Castle Archives, Survey of the manor of Dorking, MD2341 / 26 May 1608. Several published sources give this figure as £280, but my transcriptionist, Simon Neal, jotted it down as £180 when he examined the original document at Arundel Castle, Sussex.

came on the *Mayflower* to Plymouth in 1620 with his wife Alice and two children, Priscilla and Joseph, leaving behind in Dorking his married children Sarah and William. Theories regarding the possible identity of the wife or wives of William Mullins will be discussed later. He died on 21 February 1620/1 during the first winter at Plymouth,[45] and his wife Alice and son Joseph died shortly thereafter, leaving William's orphan daughter Priscilla at Plymouth.

Children of William Mullins:
- i WILLIAM MULLINS, b. say 1596. He m. in England, say 1617, a woman whose name has not been discovered. He was living in Duxbury, Mass., by 2 Oct. 1637, when Edward Hawes was granted 10 acres of land "next to William Mullens on the south side."[46] He is enumerated under the town of Duxbury on the 1643 list of men able to bear arms in Plymouth Colony.[47] There was a William Mullins who married an ANN BELL in Boston on 7 May 1656, which may be a late-in-life remarriage.

  With his 1st wife, he had three children recorded in the Dorking parish registers: 1. *Elizabeth Mullins*, bp. 26 March 1618, bur. Dorking, 15 Jan. 1620/1. 2. *Ruth Mullins*, bp. 31 Oct. 1619; no further record found. 3. *Sarah Mullins*, bp. 5 May 1622. She m. three times in New England, (1) THOMAS GANNETT, (2) WILLIAM SAVILL, and (3) THOMAS FAXON. Her will, dated 13 Aug. 1694 and proved 25 Nov. 1697 at Braintree, Mass., mentions no children from any of her three marriages.[48]

The costs and time involved in returning to Arundel Castle just to double-check the selling price was not deemed worthwhile, so I simply note the discrepancy here.

[45] Thomas Prince, *A Chronological History of New England in the Form of Annals* (1736; repr. Boston, 1826), 184. Prince records: "February 21. Die Mr. William White, Mr. William Mullins, with two more. And the 25th dies Mary, the wife of Mr. Isaac Allerton," and cites as his source "In octavo – A register of Governor Bradford's, in his own hand, recording some of the first deaths, marriages and punishments, at Plymouth." This register has never been found or transcribed, so Prince is our only source as to what was contained therein.

[46] Shurtleff and Pulsifer, *Plym. Col. Recs.*, 1:66. William Mullins was also granted ten acres of land on 6 April 1640, "lying crosse Greens Harbour Path, between the lands of Edmond Hawes and John Tisdall" (Shurtleff and Pulsifer, *Plym. Col. Recs.*, 1:146).

[47] Shurtleff and Pulsifer, *Plym. Col. Recs.*, 8:190.

[48] This family is treated in more detail in George Ernest Bowman, "The Estates of William Mullins and his Daughter Sarah (Mullins) (Gannett) (Savill) Faxon and of Her Three Husbands," MD 7(1905):37-48, 179-83.

ii (poss.) ELIZABETH MULLINS, bp. Holy Trinity, Guildford, 11 Dec. 1598. If she is indeed the daughter of William Mullins the *Mayflower* passenger, then she likely d. young, as she is not mentioned in her father's will of 1621.

iii SARAH MULLINS, b. say 1600. She was m. by 1621 to a man of the surname BLUNDEN. No further records have yet been discovered that relate to Sarah, her marriage, or any possible children. A variant of the surname, BLUNDELL, is found occasionally in Dorking. Thomas Blundell was apparently a neighbor of widow Susan Bothell in 1651, and Susan was living in the house formerly owned by William Mullins.[49] It would therefore seem quite probable this Thomas Blundell is somehow related to Sarah (Mullins) Blunden. No useful or supporting records, however, were found that could contribute anything further to our knowledge.

iv PRISCILLA MULLINS, b. say 1602; m. Plymouth in 1622 or 1623 to *Mayflower* passenger JOHN ALDEN. They had ten children.[50]

v JOSEPH MULLINS, b. say 1604. He d. sometime during the first winter at Plymouth, after his father's death on 21 Feb. 1620/1.

MULLINS-BROWNE CONNECTIONS IN DORKING, SURREY

With the Surrey records relating to William Mullins now thoroughly examined, it is possible to observe several family and social connections between the Mullins and Browne families of Dorking. The first and most obvious relates to the widow Jane Hammon, who named William Mullins an overseer of her estate. Widow Jane Hammon was the mother of John Hammon, who married Jane Browne, Peter Browne's sister, on 29 June 1610 at Dorking. She mentions both son John and daughter-in-law Jane in her will.[51] Widow Jane Hammon's other surviving child, daughter Susan, married Ephraim Bothell on 6 October 1606 in Dorking. Ephraim Bothell is the man to whom William Mullins sold his manor holdings in May 1619.

---

[49] Arundel Castle Archives, Rental of Dorking Manor, A504/1651.

[50] For information on John Alden and his descendants, see Esther L. Woodworth-Barnes, comp., *Mayflower Families for Five Generations: Vol. 16: John Alden*, ed. Alicia Crane Williams, 2 pts. to date (Plymouth, Mass., 1999-).

[51] Will of Jane Hammon, Archdeaconry of Surrey, DW/PA/7/9 ff 135v-136r; DW/PA/5/1615/56.

MARGARET (SYMONS) (DENDY) WOOD OF DORKING

The next apparent Browne-Mullins connection is found in the 1597 will of Thomas Browne, mentioned above. The witnesses to the will were John Dendy and William Symons. John Dendy and William Symons were brothers-in-law: William's sister Margaret had married John Dendy about 1576. Margaret (Symons) Dendy was widowed in 1601/2, and remarried to John Wood in Dorking on 23 July 1605; [his] will was witnessed by William Mullins in 1612.

John and Margaret (Symons) Dendy become even more interesting when we note that they had a daughter named Priscilla about 1589. John Dendy's eldest son William was a member of William Mullins's frankpledge in 1605 – and William Dendy also had a daughter named Priscilla.

WILLIAM WOOD OF DORKING

Yet another apparent Browne-Mullins association occurred in 1621, when Thomas Browne's children Michael and John sold their tenements to William Wood, as mentioned earlier. William Wood was a member of William Mullins's frankpledge in 1605, and was then apparently the successor to Mullins as tithingman the subsequent year. The will of Agnes Shore of Dorking, widow, dated 20 February 1625/6 and proved on 6 April 1626, mentions Elizabeth daughter of William Wood, butcher.[52] An overseer of her estate was Ephraim Bothell, and also mentioned are Thomas Wood and his wife Dorothy and daughter Anne. Perhaps one of these men is the "goodman Wood" mentioned in William Mullins's will, although it could just as easily have been one of John Wood's children, say son John Wood [Jr.], who was married to Ephraim Bothell's sister Susan. A William Wood was buried in Dorking on 16 November 1645, aged 76.

SOME THEORIES ON THE WIFE OR WIVES OF WILLIAM MULLINS

One of the most vexatious mysteries surrounding William Mullins is the identity of his wife or wives. Two widely published but undocumented claims exist about the identity of wife Alice, who accompanied him on the *Mayflower*. The most common of the two claims is that she was Alice

---

[52] Will of Agnes Shore, Archdeaconry of Surrey, DW/PA//5/1626/106.

Atwood. Since there is no documentation to support this claim, it is anyone's guess how it may have originated. Perhaps someone noted the "goodman Wood" in William Mullins's will, and, knowing that there was a Wood/Atwood family in early Plymouth, jumped to a conclusion. Or perhaps someone saw but failed to document the will of John Wood of Dorking, and assumed that Mullins must have married one of John Wood's daughters. But John Wood of Dorking did not have a daughter named Alice, so that squashes that theory.

Another claim that has been thrown around is that William Mullins's wife was named Alice Poretiers. This appears in Clarence Torrey's *New England Marriages Prior to 1700*.[53] Nobody has ever been able to discover what Torry used as a source for this claim. One possibility may be that he encountered the 1601 marriage of Thomas Wood to Alice Peeter (sometimes Porter) at Abinger, Surrey, a neighboring parish to Dorking.[54] If Alice Wood were widowed, she would make a potential second wife for William. Unfortunately, there are literally dozens of potential candidates in Dorking named Alice, in spite of the absence of baptism records there between 1572 and 1578.

One very interesting candidate for a wife of William Mullins would be Alice, the widow of Thomas Browne. Widowed in 1597, she could reasonably have remarried William Mullins around 1604. If this premise is correct, it would make her the second wife of William Mullins, and not the mother of his children. It would also apparently make her the aunt of *Mayflower* passenger Peter Browne, and would provide the family connection explaining his association with the Hammon family.

It was suggested earlier that William Mullins may have removed from Dorking for a time, to the vicinity of the parishes of Stoke-near-Guildford, and Holy Trinity, Guildford. Following William Mullins's name on the 1596 muster list for Stoke-near-Guildford is a man named Thomas Hammon. And at Holy Trinity, Guildford, there is an interesting marriage for a William Coolman to Annes Hammon on 15 November 1562 – a marriage which resulted in a child named Priscilla Coolman baptized on 9 March 1578/9 at that church. Because of the name *Priscilla* and her connection to a Hammon family, she

---

[53] Clarence A. Torrey, *New England Marriages Prior to 1700* (Baltimore, 1985), 526.
[54] IGI Parish Register abstract, batch M013371.

might make an interesting candidate for a first wife of William Mullins. No will for William Coolman was found in the Archdeaconry of Surrey.

Holy Trinity, Guildford, has another interesting family, headed by a James Gardinar. The will of James Gardinar of Guildford, butcher, dated 27 November 1596 and proved on 11 May 1597, names (among others) a servant Alice Dendy. The will was witnessed by George Hammon.[55] James Gardinar's son William married Alice Dendy on 26 September 1597 at Holy Trinity. Another of James Gardinar's children, James, married Sarah Hammon in November 1601 at Holy Trinity. And James Gardinar's daughter Elizabeth married John Mason there on 28 May 1604. The *Dendy, Hammon*, and *Mason* surnames all occur together at Holy Trinity, Guildford, and those families all appear to be associated with each other in Dorking as witnesses and overseers of the wills of Jane Hammon and John Wood. If it is a coincidence, it is certainly a bizarre one.

James Gardinar also had a son named Richard Gardinar, baptized on 2 February 1587 at Holy Trinity, Guildford, who was bequeathed £40 in his father's will. There was a *Mayflower* passenger of the same name who has usually (but tentatively) been identified as the Richard Gardinar baptized on 12 February 1582 at Harwich, Essex, son of John and Lucy (Russell) Gardinar – based on the fact that Lucy Russell was step-aunt of *Mayflower* master Christopher Jones. Richard Gardinar is reported by William Bradford to have become a seaman after leaving Plymouth Colony. This particular Richard Gardinar, however, if he has ties to other *Mayflower* passengers such as William Mullins and Peter Browne, might also make a reasonable candidate.

Caleb Johnson of Vancouver, Wash., is author and programmer of the MayflowerHistory.com *website. He published a book entitled* The Mayflower and Her Passengers *in 2006. This abridged article is reprinted by permission of the author and* TAG (americangenealogist.com).

---

[55] Will of James Gardinar, Archdeaconry of Surrey, DW/PA/5/1597/43.

The weaver, the shoemaker and the mother of a nation

Appendix 4

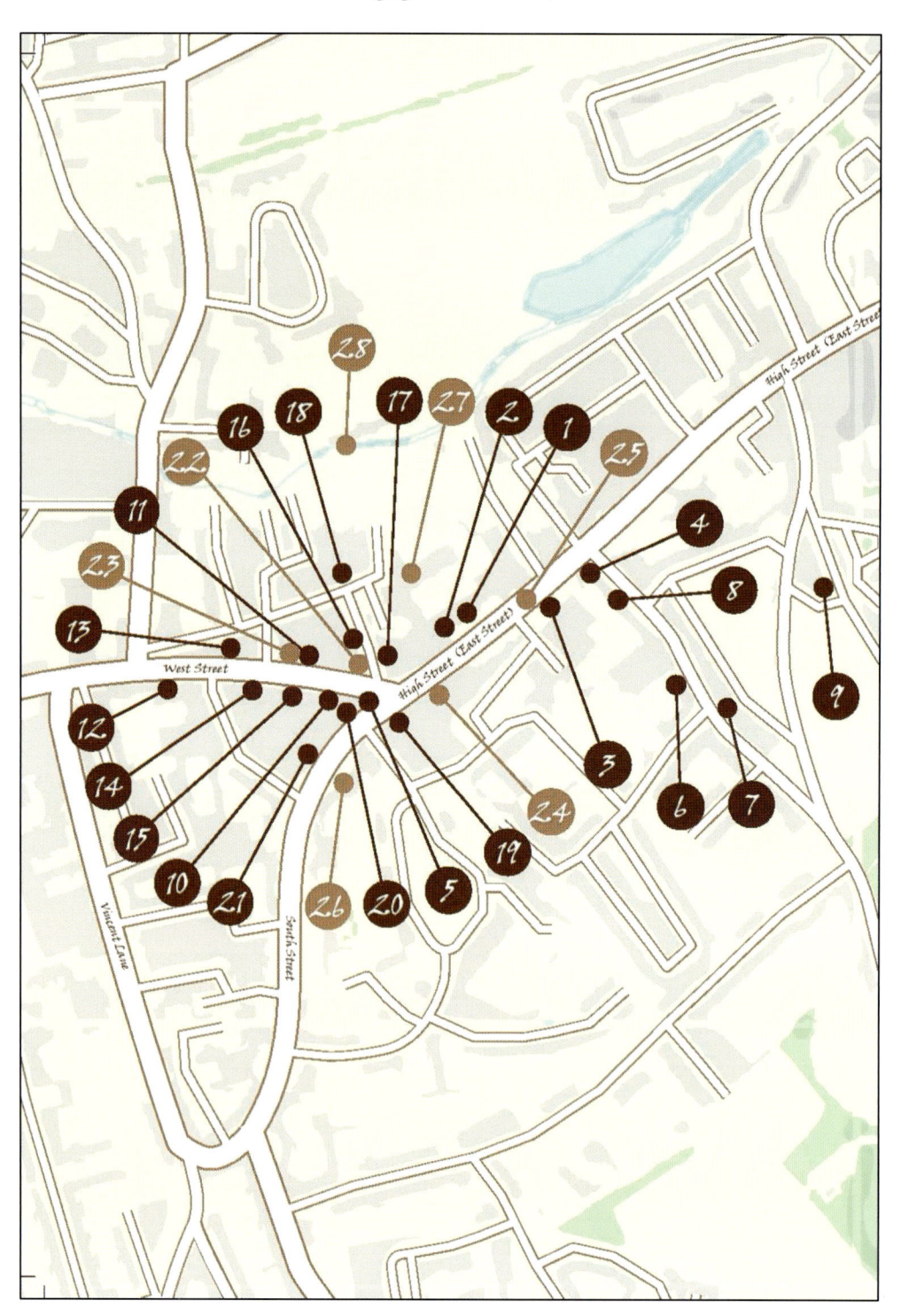

Central Dorking structures from Mullins' time which survive

(Some survive only in part as many timber framed buildings have been re-fronted or subsumed into later structures).

High Street
1. No 47 The Lemon Tree (formerly the George Inn). (Interior)
2. No 37-39 Whole Food Shop (formerly the Wheatsheaf)
3. No 138-146 The White Horse (and former Dutch House). (Interior)
4. No 170-172 Café Rouge (overhanging structure to the rear only)
5. The pump at Pump Corner

Dene Street
6. No 35-38
7. No 27-28 Pear Tree Cottage
8. No 63 (formerly a bakery)
9. No 12-13 Cotmandene (interior)

West Street
10. No 2-4 Salt Pig (interior)
11. No 58-60 Mullins' House
12. No 24 The Old House at Home (interior)
13. No 45 The Kings Arms
14. No 16a New Fountain Garden (rear wing)
15. No 11 Christique (formerly the Rose and Crown). (interior)

North Street
16. No 1 Bourneside Gallery (formerly The Gun Inn; in Mullins' time the King's Arms)
17. No 18 King's Head courtyard (formerly the old Kings Head; in Mullins' time The Lower Chequers)

Church Street
18. Leslie Cottage

South Street
19. No 7. (Interior)
20. No 8-10 St Catherine's Hospice Shop
21. No 40 Friths Chemist. (interior)

Locations or important structures from Mullins' time which do not survive
22. No 45-46 West Street HSBC (formerly The Queen's/King's Arms)
23. No 57 West Street (the premises of a butcher, linen draper and tanner; later the Bell Hotel)
24. No 20-28 High Street Robert Dyas (formerly the Chequers Inn)
25. The Old Market Hall in the centre of the High Street
26. Butter Hill (the site of the home of William Henn, supplier of butter to the court of Henry VIII)
27. St Martin's Church
28. Pippbrook (the communal washing area)

The weaver, the shoemaker and the mother of a nation

Bibliography

Baker, Peggy M: 'Priscilla's Choice', The Compact, 2014

Bradford, William: Of Plymouth Plantation (1630-51, published 1854)

Bragg, Melvyn: The Adventure of English, 2003

Bryson, Bill: Made in America, 1998

Charlton, Warwick: The Voyage of the *Mayflower* II, 1957

Ettlinger, Vivien: 'Mullins' or Sheffields'?', Dorking History 2012

Ettlinger, Vivien et al: Dorking: a Surrey market town through twenty centuries, 1991

Hunter, Pam: William Mullins, Pilgrim Father, 2000

Johnson, Caleb H: The *Mayflower* and her passengers, 2006

Johnson, Caleb H: 'The Probable English Origin of *Mayflower* Passenger Peter Browne and His Association with *Mayflower* Passenger William Mullins', The American Genealogist, 2004

Longfellow, Henry Wadsworth 'The Courtship of Miles Standish', 1858

Russell, Conrad (ed): The Origins of the English Civil War, 1984

Stratton, Eugene Aubrey: Plymouth Colony; Its History and People, 1620-1691, 1986

Walker, John EN: Nos. 58-61 West Street, Dorking (leaflet)

Winslow, Edward: A Relation or Journal of the Proceedings of the English Plantation at Plymouth, 1622

The weaver, the shoemaker and the mother of a nation

Index

Adams, John 54, 56
Adams, John Quincy 54
Alden, John
    early life 44
    voyage 25, 30, 60
    marriage 44-47
    later life 50-53
Alden, John Jr 56-57
Anne, the 50
Bothell, Ephraim 7, 16, 70, 73, 75, 76
Bradford, William 20, 30, 32, 37, 39, 44, 60, 78
Brewster, William 20, 30, 36, 41, 51, 60
Brown, Mary 51
Browne family 11, 15, 66-69
Browne, John 51, 66
Browne, Peter 7, 17, 23, 28, 30, 33-34, 41, 50-51, 60, 64-69, 75, 77, 78
Cardinal's Hat, the 11
Carter, Robert 24, 28, 30, 36, 40, 60, 62, 70
Carver, John 22, 30, 35, 36, 62, 69, 70
Chitty, Edward 13
Coddington, Hannah & Stockdale 51
Courtship of Miles Standish, the 44-48
Cushman, Robert 22, 24, 26
Dorking 8, 9
    Cotmandene 4
    Holmwood Common 9
    inns 10
    Pump Corner 4, 6, 10
    streets 9
Dudley, Jane & William 51
Dutch House, the 11
Elizabeth I 15, 16, 20, 21
Ford, Martha 41, 50, 51, 64
Fortune, the 41, 50, 64
George Inn, the 11
Goodwin, Edward 12
Gun Inn, the 11, 12
Harding, Phoebe 51, 66

Heale, Giles 62, 69
Hussey, Christopher 51
Jacob, the 56
James I 28, 29
    court 16-17
    religious convictions 15
Jones, Christopher 24, 30, 35, 40, 62, 69
King's Arms, the 8, 10, 11, 12, 14
King's Head, the 11
Leslie Cottage 11, 13
Little James, the 50
Longfellow, Henry Wadsworth 44, 46, 47
Lower Chequers, the 11
Mary I 15, 16
Mayflower, the 4, 7, 17, 20, 21
    history 24
    dimensions 24, 27
    chartering 22
    passenger list 60-61
    voyage 25-27, 52
    return 33, 35, 40, 45
Mayflower Compact, the 28-30, 32, 45, 53, 64
Merchant Adventurers 22, 23, 35, 40, 41, 50, 62
Mullins, Alice 6, 7, 24, 35, 40, 61, 62, 66, 69, 73, 76-77
Mullins, Joseph 6, 7, 24, 35, 40, 61, 62, 66, 70, 73
Mullins, Priscilla 6, 7, 24, 35, 40, 41, 61, 62, 66, 70, 73
    marriage 44-47
    children 48-51, 53-56
Mullins, Sarah (Blunden) 6, 35, 36, 53, 62, 63, 69, 73
Mullins, Sarah 52-53
Mullins, William 4, 5, 11, 14, 16, 61, 66
    early life 4, 15, 70-73
    family 6, 72, 76
    property 4, 5, 6, 7, 10, 12, 15, 73
    Mayflower 23, 24, 28, 30, 54
    religion 17
    death 34-34, 36, 37, 40, 62-63,

Mullins, William Jr 6, 35, 36, 52-53, 62, 63, 69, 73
Old House, the 11
Pear Tree Cottage 11, 13
Plymouth colony
    Plimouth Rock 32
    New Plymouth 32-33, 37, 50-51
    Duxbury 51-53
Queen's Arms, the –
    see King's Arms
Raleigh, Sir Walter 20
Ray, Charles 47
Religious beliefs 15-16, 20
    in Holland 20-23, 36
Rose and Crown, the 11, 18
Salem witch trials 57
Samoset 39
Settlement of the Americas 20
    pre-European 32-33
    Jamestown colony 21, 22, 37, 38
    Roanoke settlement 20, 37
    later settlement 57
Sheffield family 6, 73
Shoemaking 4, 5
Speedwell, the 25, 26
Standish, Myles 25, 30, 37, 44-45, 50, 51, 52, 53, 61
St Martin's church 7, 15, 16

Thanksgiving 42
Tisquantum ('Squanto') 39
Upper Chequers, the 11
Weston, Thomas 22, 24
Wheatsheaf, the 18
White Horse, the 11
White, Susannah 34, 40, 61
Winslow, Edward 30, 40, 41, 42, 52, 61

Current Titles from The Cockerel Press

A History of Brockham Park: from Gentleman's Residence to Award Winning Laboratory by Albert Bird

A History of St Paul's School by Helen Wharmby

Dorking's Famous Caves: History, Mystery and Geology by Professor Richard Selley

Early Medieval Dorking 600-1200 AD by Susannah Horne

Mole Valley Open Gardens by David Drummond

The Dorking Cockerel (booklet)

The Museum Guide to Dorking: a Brief History of the Town and Surrounding Villages by Kathy Atherton

The Tillingbourne Valley by George E Collins

The Villages of Abinger Common and Wotton by Terry O'Kelly

Time Gentlemen, Please: the Story of Dorking Pubs by David Langford and Jim Docking

Suffragettes, Suffragists & Antis: the fight for the vote in the Surrey Hills by Kathy Atherton

The Rob Walker Racing Team – Dorking's part in motor racing history by Tom Loftus

The Rob Walker Centenary Festival by Tom Loftus

Lonesome Lodge: A Lost Palladian Villa by Capel History Group

Dorking, a town underground by Sam Dawson

The Vanishing River of Box Hill by Peter Brown

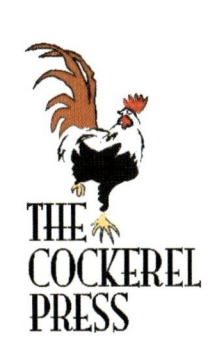

THE COCKEREL PRESS

The weaver, the shoemaker and the mother of a nation